This book is dedicated to all coaches and players
who want to improve their game

**Library of Congress
Cataloging - in - Publication Data**

Game Vision in Soccer
by Mick Critchell, Jark Bosma and Keith Granger

ISBN-13: 978-1-59164-115-5
ISBN-10: 1-59164-115-2
Library of Congress Control Number: 2008938861

Contents

Symbols

The symbols used throughout the exercises and diagrams may be identified in the following representative Key table:

Symbol	Description
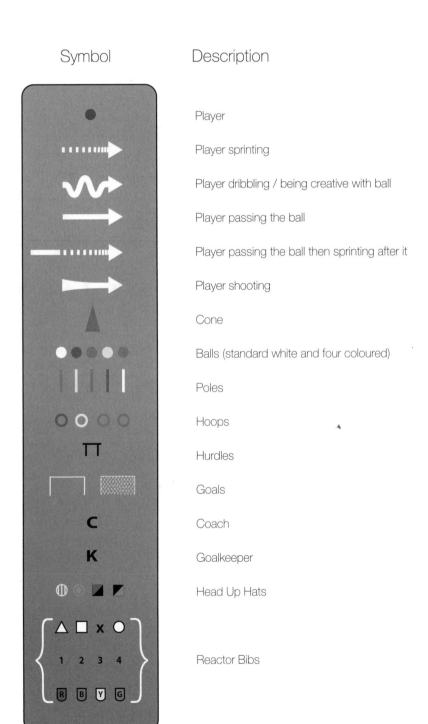	Player
	Player sprinting
	Player dribbling / being creative with ball
	Player passing the ball
	Player passing the ball then sprinting after it
	Player shooting
	Cone
	Balls (standard white and four coloured)
	Poles
	Hoops
	Hurdles
	Goals
	Coach
	Goalkeeper
	Head Up Hats
	Reactor Bibs

Mick's Foreword

For some time, Keith and I had been trying to think up practices and devise equipment which would help young players get their heads away from the ball to the surrounding area. With this in mind, we created the 'head up hat' and 'reactor bibs' with geometric shapes and numbers on them and developed practices which used different coloured footballs or different shaped pitches.

At the same time, we became aware that several professional clubs were using computer programmes as a means of enhancing visual awareness and peripheral vision. I was able to access one of these programmes and can honestly say the only thing I gained from it was a headache. I could not see how a computer programme would, in any way, improve visual awareness or peripheral vision in a fast-moving game such as football. In fact, as football players are rarely looking straight ahead - but up, down and side to side, whilst often using their peripheral vision to keep an eye on the ball - just following arrows on a screen seemed counter-productive to me.

The only way forward I could see on vision training was to provide practical exercises which could be used on the training ground. At the time, I had nothing to substantiate my opinion, but then I was lucky enough to meet Jark and Bo, who brought their son Bouwe to the Football Garage. Jark is a brain surgeon and Bo a neuropsychologist, so they were the ideal couple to talk to on the subject. In fact, I made their life hell by badgering them for months, trying to get as much information as possible on vision training and the working of the brain. Fortunately, they both agreed on our approach to coaching and felt that unless players were always put in game situations, where decisions were continually made, then the practice was of little value. They had already taken Bouwe to various training sessions, but usually came away disappointed because most of the training they observed had little relevance to the game. They could not see how training without decision-making was going to make Bouwe a better player.

It was from this background that I got the idea to write a book on vision training for football. I asked Jark to write the theoretical section, leaving Keith and I to concentrate on the practical aspects of coaching vision training, with the help of Joe Griffin, an ex-pupil of mine and an expert on functional strength and balance. We feel the book will provide players with an opportunity to improve their visual awareness, visual scanning speed and peripheral vision, which will in turn enable them to react more quickly and make faster and more accurate decisions in most football situations. Good vision will tell the rest of the body what to do, as a result of what it has seen. I am just so grateful that Jark and Bo decided to bring their son to the Football Garage, because their support, encouragement and words of wisdom have given me the confidence that the way we work is the way forward in vision training for football.

Jark's Foreword

When Mick approached me to ask if I would contribute to this book, my first reaction was one of surprise: why me? I had never been 'involved' with football before, and I knew little about training methods. My involvement in football thus far had been seeing my children - both passionate football players - play.

In the past, kids, like many old football heroes such as Johan Cruyff, learned to play through lots of practice on the street, at school and in the park. Unfortunately, urbanisation reduced the number of places children could go to kick a ball about and kids were not allowed to play on the street anymore. Gradually a more scientific approach to training was developed, but children could not put this into practice regularly. It is now time to move on and combine theory and practice. The more practice, the better the player will become. We have, however, remained stuck with predominantly skill training. Vision in the game, or game sense, is poorly taught. This is where Mick had some very good ideas.

As he explained to me what he was actually seeking, namely a more scientific explanation to support his ideas, I agreed. After all, everything he suggested for exercises to make children better football players made perfect sense. As we talked, I realised that the scientific basis to back up his theories is there and is mostly found in basic anatomy and physiology!

It has been hard work at times, especially to fit it into a busy schedule of work and leisure, the latter mostly meaning supporting the children in their activities. However, it has been gratifying and I feel that we have succeeded in creating a book that will benefit many coaches and sportsmen, not just footballers, and that may become a platform for further improvement of training methods in the future.

Acknowledgements

I would like to thank my wife and friends, who gave up their time to make a significant contribution to this book: Joe Griffin and Rowan Vine for acting as models, Alan Duffy for taking the photographs and my wife Carol for her proof-reading and total support.

I would like to give special thanks to John Ellis and Allan Manners for their professional input and help in pulling the whole thing together.

Mick

First I want to express my gratitude to Mick for asking and encouraging me to co-write this book. His vision on the future of coaching has proved an inspiration.

I want to thank the publisher Thieme Georg Verlag for giving their permission to modify and redraw the illustrations 2, 13 and 14.

Perhaps most importantly I am very grateful for the continued support my wife has given me throughout the project and also for the invaluable contribution she has made, especially in the cognitive psychological description of the concept of memory and development of memory patterns.

Jark

I would like to thank my wife Nicky for her support and encouragement, my two sons who make me proud and bring enjoyment as I watch them develop in training using the practices in this book.

Special thanks must go to John Ellis, Huw Jennings and the Premier League for their professional guidance and friendship. Thank you to Keith Curtis for his permission to use his photographs.

Keith

Special thanks to Theo Walcott for being an excellent pupil and a great role model for all the young players of today.

PART 1

NEUROLOGICAL BASIS FOR PROPOSED EXERCISES

Introduction

This book consists of two parts. In this part, we will discuss the theory of the basic neurological science that supports the exercises proposed in the second part.

The basic principle in functional neurology is that the nervous system works by activation of effector organs e.g. eyes, ears and muscles. Every neurological function - e.g. speech, hearing or vision - is controlled by an anatomical correlate, e.g. the centre for speech, for hearing or for vision. It is obvious that none of these centres can work independently. They are centres of integration. They receive a great many stimuli (information) from other centres and process and relay a great deal to others. This is absolutely essential for a good functioning of the nervous system, indeed of the whole organism i.e. the individual.

Thus, the function of the nervous system in an individual can be assessed from the individual's behaviour. We are "behaviourist" in the study of functional neurology. As such, functional neurology can only be understood when we assume that consciousness is not the principal role of the nervous system, but only an important epiphenomenon. Indeed consciousness is also essential in the process of learning.

The simplest form of behaviour or neurological function is the reflex. The most complex form of behaviour is the word (language). The word remains an act, for example spoken or written. When the word is not effectively formulated (written or spoken) but only thought, then this is only possible because there is a 'word-act'. Functional neurology then studies the procedure of expression of thought. The contents of thought are the domain of psychology and psychiatry.

Certain activities can be learned and can develop into an automatism or a reflex without the need to think about it. This can be a very complex process and it can also be practised, for example walking, running and cycling.

In the same way, complex activities can be trained and gradually become a reflex or automatism. Many sports are an example: the technical skill of skiing, skating, throwing a javelin or hitting the ball with a tennis racket. The individual no longer has to think how to place his foot, how to hold a racket or how to hit the ball; it has become an automatism.

In team sports, observation and knowing where your team mates and opponents are, and with it awareness of position, possibilities of attack and possible danger, play a dominant role.

Players who excel are often characterised by their 'great vision' or 'great awareness' or 'instinct'. Such vision is of great importance for the success of a team. Whilst it may be true to say that there are talents who appear to have a naturally developed 'vision of the game', there is no reason to believe that such vision cannot be trained. Just like the technical skill of how to kick a ball this can be trained and gradually become an automatism. Unfortunately, the emphasis of most training is generally still on technical ability alone and this particular aspect of observation and awareness is being neglected. Yet vision exercises can be used to improve performance; visual abilities affect soccer (sport) performance and the acquisition of motor skills. Even talents who have great vision and awareness will benefit from such training and become even better players.

Exercises that concentrate on 'vision of the game' and integration of 'vision' and technical skills can contribute to the gradual development of an automatism of such. Exercises that train the observations and the best reactions to that information can help to develop the game, the 'vision of the game'. The best player will be the one who makes the correct decision most of the time, and who uses his experience to create favourable situations and to find solutions for problems he is faced with, such as responding to an opponent's attack. The exercises we describe will help to build this experience and thus to enhance 'vision of the game'.

Training or learning requires memory. Memory has various components: these include visual memory and auditory memory (memory of hearing). Vision plays a pivotal role in the game. Indeed vision provides the bulk of stimuli in team sports. Evidently visual memory is of the utmost importance for progression in training. Hence we emphasise the use of visual aids in this book.

Whereas vision exercises can improve sports performance, the exercises described in this book are taken a step farther. The exercises aim to train patterns of activities. The patterns are stored and assimilated in the memory creating 'maps'. In different situations different (trained) patterns will be 'called up' from the memory. Indeed, well practised and often recalled information is stored in deep (or tertiary) memory from where it can be recalled quickly. The best player is the one who in all different situations applies the best or most useful patterns and who, through association, develops new patterns for himself. In other words, the intelligent player builds on learned patterns to develop new ones for new situations he is faced with in the game. The more he trains them the better he gets at doing it. This is the neurological equivalent of the instinct or vision of the game.

Whilst we agree with Evans that reading the game requires the players in a team to read the game in the same way and put their judgements into practice in a collective and consistent way, the individual player with great vision will be able to 'read' the players of his own team as well as his opponents. Indeed, developing new patterns by applying learned ones cannot be taught. It is intrinsic to the player; it is the intelligence of the player that determines that capability. However, it is clear that every player will benefit from learning these patterns and in this way will maximise their own capabilities to develop new ones. In addition, the more a player practises, the more opportunity he will have to develop new 'maps'.

Thus we come to a definition of Vision or Instinct (of the game): the capability to recognise patterns and develop new patterns to solve situations based on previously learned patterns.

In the next few chapters we will outline the basic anatomy of the nervous system that provides the 'wiring' or 'network' that makes such learning possible. With the descriptive anatomy, we will blend some functional anatomy and some neurophysiological principles.

It is an enormous subject and inevitably the following description is largely a simplification. To enhance understanding, we provide some illustrations to make it easier to see how it works. We have used layman's terms or clarified the anatomical terminology as much as possible. It is by no means necessary to try to memorise every detail. We try to explain how the underlying neurological processes work. Some understanding of this neurological 'wiring network' should suffice to offer an insight into the basic science that supports the exercises proposed in this book.

Anatomy Basics

The anatomy of the nervous system is somewhat difficult to imagine as the brain and spinal cord are solid organs; the structural pathways for conduction of stimuli lie within these and are difficult to recognise (the illustrations are therefore largely schematic). One could see it as the wiring through which all the impulses travel.

The amount of information received and processed is enormous. It is estimated that we receive approximately one billion bits per second (for comparison: one page contains approximately 1000 bits of information). We process this in the brain and become conscious of only between ten and one hundred bits every second. Visual information provides the bulk of this!

The nervous system is subdivided into a central and a peripheral nervous system. The central nervous system is again subdivided into the brain and the spinal cord.

Several major parts are recognised in the brain (Fig 1):

Brainstem — the seat for control of vital functions (breathing and circulation) and for centres of the cranial nerves that control the nervous functions to the head and neck (eye movements, hearing and balance, face muscles and sensation, tongue and throat muscles and sensations, some neck muscles). It includes the Midbrain, the centre for visual coordination.

Cerebellum — this is the small brain. It is the centre for coordination and integration of movements.

Hypothalamus — a centre essential for homeostatic (vegetative) functions, i.e. maintaining body fluid parameters at the correct levels. It also 'programs' the body by activating or inhibiting certain neurological processes and pathways to promote behaviour in favour of digestion, reproduction or activity depending on the body's need at the time.

Limbic system — this is a system the processes of which are still to a large extent unknown. It is the seat of 'Fright-Fight-Flight reactions' or emotions and possibly an important centre for initiative.

Thalamus — the centre important in the relay of stimuli.

Cortex — this is developmentally the highest part of the brain where consciousness occurs.

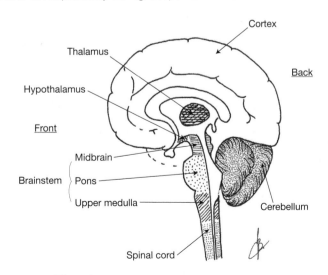

Fig 1. The major anatomical parts of the brain

Impulses or stimuli are carried through the peripheral nerves to the central nervous system. These include information from receptors in the muscles, tendons and joints on body position and muscle tone.

Via a central centre called the thalamus that mediates all perceptions except smell and pain, the stimuli can ultimately end in the cortex of the brain (the outer shell or surface) to become conscious. (Fig 2)

As such, the cortex is developmentally the 'highest' part of the brain. Not all stimuli reach the cortex however; indeed many stimuli are dealt with at a lower - subconscious - level, for example reflexes. The nervous system will process the information and generate a response to the stimuli that is carried back through the peripheral nerves to the effector organs, e.g. the musculoskeletal system, heart, lungs, bowels etc. (Fig 3)

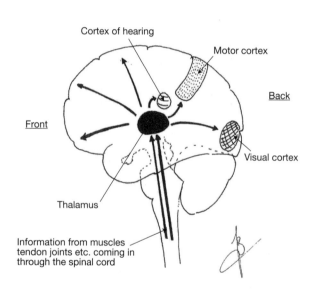

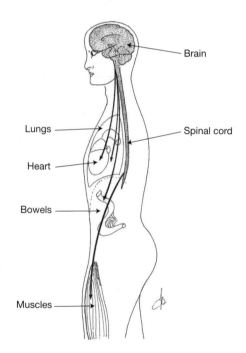

Fig 2. **The Thalamus. An important centre that relays most stimuli. (Modified and redrawn, with permission, from Silbernagl and Despopoulos: Sesam Atlas van de Fysiologie, Bosch en Keuning, 1981.)**

Fig 3. **Effector responses from the central nervous system to the musculoskeletal system, heart, lungs, bowels etc.**

The cortex has a somatotopic arrangement i.e. the information received from the various parts of the body and the response signals have systematic projections on the cortex. (Fig 4A,B)

Vision provides a huge amount (the most) of stimuli of the nervous system. Not surprisingly therefore, it takes up a large part of the structures of the brain and the visual cortex (the centre of awareness of what one sees) has a huge number of connections to all centres within the nervous system. Vision of the game cannot develop without the constant stream of accurate visual information from the game itself or the pattern of play.

It is obvious that the anatomical systems must function optimally to achieve optimum performance. Indeed, visual deficiencies must be detected early as they may increase the player's risk of injury or interfere with the player's performance, for example by misplacing the ball or mistiming a tackle. Especially in younger players this may cause frustration and anger, and can lead to conflict with team-mates or the referee. For that reason and reasons outlined above we will concentrate on vision.

A.

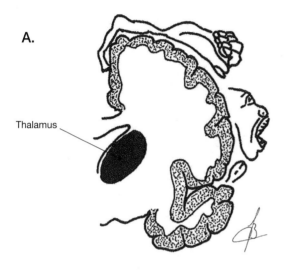

Thalamus

B.

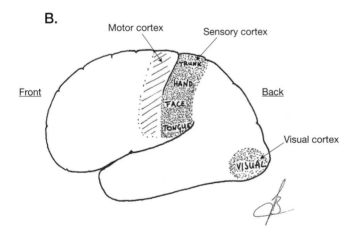

Fig 4. **Cross-section of one side of the brain (A) and side view (B) demonstrating the somatotopic arrangement of the motor cortex. Also indicated is the central location of the thalamus.**

Vision

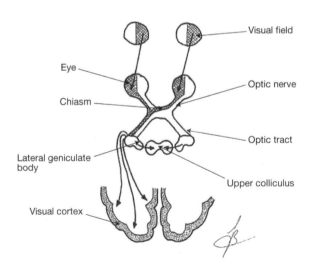

Fig 5. The visual pathways and the relay of the field of vision. The crossed area shows the rearrangement of the visual pathways such that the right visual field for each eye is relayed to the left side of the brain and vice versa.

The visual impulses from each eye are transmitted through the optic nerve (nerve from the eyeball), chiasm (a crossing of part of the optic nerves allowing reorganisation of the impulses) and optic tract to the brain. This is arranged in such a way that what we see on the left of the midline with both eyes is registered on the right side of the brain in the right visual cortex and vice versa.

These pathways have connections through the so-called lateral geniculate bodies to other centres in the midbrain. Thus the midbrain is home to some very important centres that are called the (upper) colliculi. These are the relay stations for visual reflexes. (Fig 5)

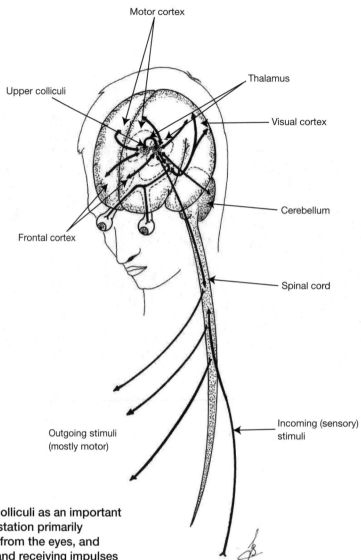

Motor cortex

Upper colliculi

Thalamus

Visual cortex

Cerebellum

Frontal cortex

Spinal cord

Outgoing stimuli
(mostly motor)

Incoming (sensory)
stimuli

Fig 6. **The upper colliculi as an important integration and relay station primarily receiving information from the eyes, and sending impulses to and receiving impulses from many other centres of the central nervous system (see text).**

As relay stations, the colliculi receive and send impulses to many (possibly all) other centres and pathways in the central nervous system. The pathways include connections with each other, with the thalamus, and with the lower colliculi (relay stations for reflexes of hearing). They receive input from these, from the brainstem which houses the centres for vital functions such as breathing, and also from nerve tracts from the spinal cord, namely the spinotectal pathways and the lateral lemniscus that carry sensory impulses (touch and pain, joint position sense). Vice versa, they send impulses to the other colliculi, to the thalamus, to the spinal cord via the tectospinal tract, and to the cerebellum and brain stem via the tectocerebellar and tectobulbar tract respectively. Indeed the colliculi form an important integration system. (Fig 6)

As mentioned above the thalamus mediates all perception except smell and pain and relays stimuli to and from the cortex, including the visual stimuli. It relays the quality of the perception and also sends it to other deep centres in the brain, the pallidum and the hypothalamus. These mediate visceral and somatosensory reactions, i.e. non-voluntary reactions from organs and from the body (musculoskeletal reactions), for example, stiffen when startled, getting goose pimples, and feeling sick when confronted with certain images.

Vision & Balance

The course of the vestibular (balance) pathways is not exactly known. As the vestibular (balance) organ is intrinsically linked with hearing and the impulses for balance and hearing travel within the same nerve (the vestibulocochlear nerve), albeit in functionally different bundles, it is very likely that they have very similar connections in the nervous system.

There are known significant connections with centres in the cortex that control global movement, including area 8 for voluntary movements and eye movements and area 19 for reflex adaptation. Area 19 is a visual association area. (Fig 7)

Impulses generated in the vestibular (balance) organs in the inner ear travel through the vestibulo-cochlear nerve to the vestibular (balance) centres in the brainstem. From there they are relayed to the centres for control of eye movements in the brainstem, to the cerebellum (small brain), to the cortex (the post central gyrus, centre for spatial orientation) and to the spinal cord. This provokes reactions or reflexes mostly aimed at maintaining balance and at eye movements (keeping an eye on the surroundings). (Fig 8)

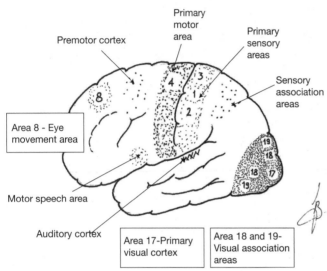

Premotor cortex
Primary motor area
Primary sensory areas
Sensory association areas

Area 8 - Eye movement area

Motor speech area

Auditory cortex

Area 17-Primary visual cortex

Area 18 and 19- Visual association areas

Fig 7. **Side view (left) of the brain. The organisation of the cortex in functionally different areas. These are numbered. The principal areas are indicated.**

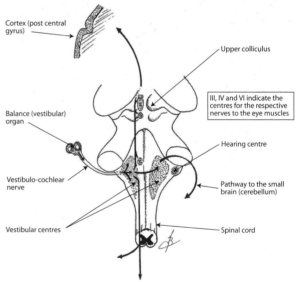

Cortex (post central gyrus)

Upper colliculus

III, IV and VI indicate the centres for the respective nerves to the eye muscles

Balance (vestibular) organ

Hearing centre

Vestibulo-cochlear nerve

Pathway to the small brain (cerebellum)

Vestibular centres

Spinal cord

Fig 8. **View of the brainstem from behind (small brain removed) demonstrating the pathways for information from the balance organ.**

Equally importantly, there are connections with the centres that coordinate motor function. (Fig 9) These include the cerebellum (small brain), and the extrapyramidal system. The latter is so-called to distinguish it from the pyramidal system that is responsible for voluntary movements. It plays a role in muscle tone, in resistance to passive movements thereby smoothing overall movements (synergism or the control of movement of opposing muscles), it controls automatic and semi-automatic instinctive movements - for example picking up an object which is a sequence of movements - that are initiated in the Pallidum (a deep control centre) and it is responsible for fine, specific and precise movements. It has numerous feedback loops to many, if not all, other centres. Defects in the extrapyramidal system are exemplified by Parkinson's disease, which is mostly known for significant tremor and shaking.

The cerebellum (small brain) receives impulses from the vestibular (balance) centres. It sends pathways to the same and to the spinal cord (cerebellospinal tract) and from there to the thalamus to influence controlled movements. (Fig 10)

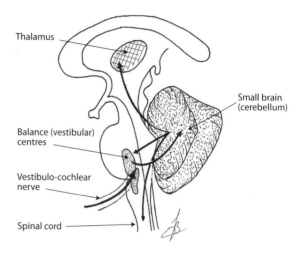

Fig 10. Pathways from the small brain (cerebellum) after receiving information from the balance (vestibular) centres.

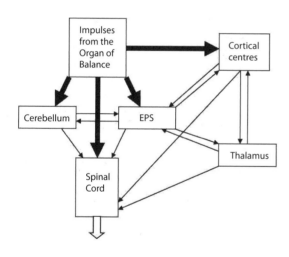

Fig 9. A schematic illustration of some of the connections involved in a response to impulses from the organ of balance (EPS = extrapyramidal system). See text for explanation.

Apart from the mostly subconscious reactions to coordinate eye movements, the body responds by and large to the information received and processed by the brain through muscular activity or movements. Two main mechanisms can be distinguished: the motor-move system or voluntary motor function (see below under VISUAL PERCEPTION AND MOVEMENT), and the motor-hold system or the postural motor system. The latter is responsible for balance and for the body's position in its environment. It is also known as sensorimotor function as it depends on continuous flow of sensory impulses.

Simple spinal reflexes such as the tendon reflexes and other more complex muscular reflexes play an important role in the motor-hold system. They are controlled via spinal pathways by motor centres in the brainstem. The centres receive their information from the organs of balance, from the joint position sensors of the neck, from the cerebellum (small brain), the eyes (visual cortex) ears and nose (organ of smell or olfactory organ). They are the relay station for position and stance reflexes. (Fig 11) Their function is to maintain body position and balance, obviously important in sports.

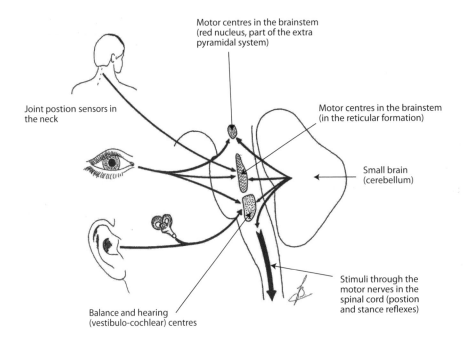

Motor centres in the brainstem (red nucleus, part of the extra pyramidal system)

Joint position sensors in the neck

Motor centres in the brainstem (in the reticular formation)

Small brain (cerebellum)

Stimuli through the motor nerves in the spinal cord (postion and stance reflexes)

Balance and hearing (vestibulo-cochlear) centres

Fig 11. **Pathways that play an important role in position and stance reflexes as part of the motor-hold system.**

Visual Perception & Movement

The conscious awareness of what we see around us (vision) is what makes it possible to perceive movement and plan our own movements. As we saw, the awareness of vision is located in the visual cortex. The cortex is highly specialised and different areas have different functions that are important to the perception of movement. These areas cater for colour, shape, and orientation. A separate area is involved in tracking or perception of movement (area V5) (Fig 12). This area receives input from the primary visual cortex. Within this area neurons are grouped and so highly specialised as to be sensitive to movement in a particular direction. Centres in the deeper centres of the brain and the superior colliculi are also involved in perception of movement.

Thus information - or neural impulses - is constantly received and processed. Signals are sent from the visual cortex to centres that control movement, voluntary and involuntary, conscious and subconscious. Amongst the areas that also receive input is the medial superior temporal lobe that analyses the information about movement and distance to objects. It houses the centre for spatial awareness. (Fig 12)

Spatial awareness is obviously very important in any sporting activity, for example in sailing to judge the distance to a mark and to other boats, in football to find space and judge the distance to pass a ball, in tennis to judge the time needed to get to the ball, in javelin throwing to judge the distance to the line etc. Vision plays a pivotal role in spatial awareness and movement.

The motor-move system allows the execution of purposeful movements. It includes the thinking about the movements, i.e. the voluntary movements. As indicated above, it is not a system working in isolation (no system does) but rather a system that is closely linked with the motor-hold system. Many nervous centres are part of it including centres in the cortex, basal centres, thalamus, cerebellum, brainstem and the spinal cord. The pathways for this system are only partly known.

In short, when a decision - conscious or subconscious - is taken for a particular movement a signal is generated in the subcortical areas (areas immediately under the cortex). (Fig 13A) The signal travels to an area called the associative cortex which 'constructs' the movement, i.e. it generates the signals needed to make the movement happen. (Fig 13B) These travel to the cerebellum and to the basal centres. (Fig 13C, Programming) The basal centres control the slower global movement whereas the cerebellum controls the coordination of the faster and finer movements. Via the thalamus the signals travel to the motor cortex (Fig 13D, Relay of signals) which then 'fires' the instructions to the musculoskeletal system through the motor nerves in the pyramidal tract to the spinal cord and peripheral nerves. (Fig 13E, command to move) There is a constant sensory feedback during the process that modifies the signal helping to adjust the final movement. (Fig 13F)

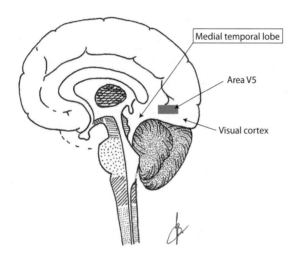

Medial temporal lobe

Area V5

Visual cortex

Fig 12. **Inside (medial) view of the brain showing the close relationship between visual cortex and medial temporal lobe.**

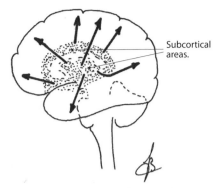

A. Decision to kick the ball. Signals a rise in the subcortical areas and travel to the associative cortex.

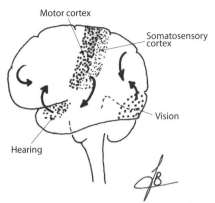

B. Construction of movement. "Here is how to kick".

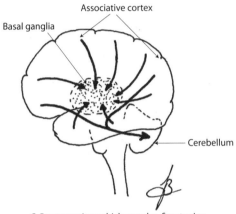

C. Programming: which muscles, fine-tuning, how much power/strength.

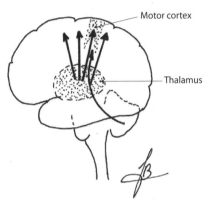

D. Relay of signals via the thalamus to the motor cortex (and also the premotor and supplementary motor areas).

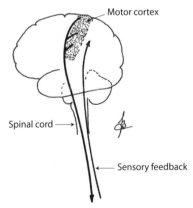

E. Command to move. Signal sent from the motor cortex to the muscles

F. Execution of movement: kicking the ball

Fig 13. **The sequence of processes involved in the execution of movement. (Modified and redrawn, with permission, from Silbernagl and Despopoulos: Color Atlas of Physiology, 5th Ed. Georg Thieme Verlag, 2003.)**

Vision, Balance & Movement Together

The importance of the motor-hold and motor-move systems can be illustrated by the example of a football player striking the ball. (Fig 14)

When the ball is passed the player receiving the ball moves his body towards the ball (target). This is a function of the motor-move system. He ensures adequate support on one leg whilst counterbalancing with his upper limbs and upper body. That is a function of the motor-hold system. The player keeps an eye on the ball, a function of the centres for eye movement control and coordination, whilst the visual cortex analyses the speed and course of the ball. The associative cortex then prepares the response, i.e. the movement of kicking the ball, including the force and slicing, spinning or lifting, for which both systems come into action again.

Fig 14. **The motor-hold and motor-move system working together when a football player strikes the ball (see text). (Modified and redrawn, with permission, from Silbernagl and Despopoulos: Sesam Atlas van de Fysiologie, Bosch en Keuning, 1981.)**

Vision & colour

The eyeball is a sphere that is lined with nerves on the inside (retina). The human eye is in essence an intrinsic part of the brain and indeed, when we look into the eye with a special instrument (fundoscope) we look directly onto nervous tissue, the retina.

The nerve cells of the retina are light sensors cells. The range of sensitivity of light perception (visual spectrum) is from 400 nm (violet) to 700 nm (red). There are two types of light sensor cells: rods and cones. (Fig 15)

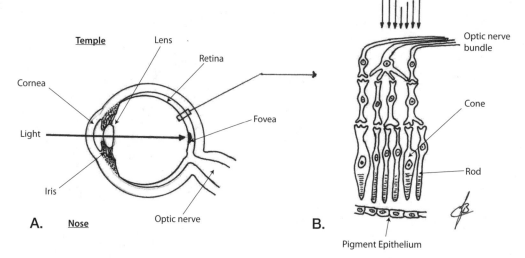

Fig 15. Horizontal cross-section through the eye (A). At zero degrees the light falls directly onto the Fovea Centralis. The Fovea has almost exclusively cones for sharp vision. The small box enlarged demonstrates the structure of the retina (B), which is the innermost lining of the eyeball that 'collects' all the information (light) and sends the stimuli to the cortex via the optic nerve and visual pathways.

Cones have peak sensitivities for the colours blue (wavelength 450 nm), red (580 nm) and green (540 nm). The sensitivity of rods is centred around 550 nm (yellow-green), which means no perception of colour.

The rods and cones are arranged in a certain way; centrally around an area called the fovea is a concentration of cones whereas more peripherally there are only rods. (Fig 15 and 16)

This arrangement allows for the perception of light and therefore movement from an angle of almost 180 degrees but colour vision is received at a narrower angle. At low light levels the rods become increasingly important for the perception of light (night vision). The information received by the retina (light perception) is sent to the visual cortex where it is extensively processed to produce a conscious image. (See Fig 5) This arrangement shows the importance of the light conditions; good light is essential for colour perception. It also explains why colour blindness can significantly hinder a player in his game. It is important that the condition - like any other visual impairment - is diagnosed at a young age. Only then can strategies be developed, and training be targeted to overcome the disadvantage.

This capacity for colour differentiation, given the huge amount of visual information that is processed by the brain, can be exploited.

Thus, by introducing colour stimuli into game practice we can sharpen the players' awareness of other players and the space around them. This will enhance their use of space and therefore their understanding of the game. The simplest example is, of course, two teams playing in different coloured shirts.

Using different coloured hats in training can also be an invaluable aid. Indeed when practising in more difficult situations than actually seen in a match, where the players only need to look out for their own colours, the match circumstances will become relatively easy. The player can thus concentrate on creating and reacting to new situations in the game. The use of such hats will be explained in the second part of the book.

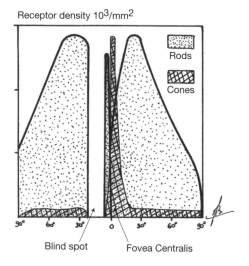

Fig 16. Diagram demonstrating the density of cones and rods concentrically around the central axis of the eyeball. The blind spot indicates the area where the optic nerve is formed. There is no light perception here.

Vision and Shape

Similar to colour stimuli, team shapes and patterns, such as triangles and diamonds that players use during the game when passing the ball around, are similarly recognised through functioning of the visual system. These patterns and shapes are recognised consciously in area V5 (see above). The action taken by the player is a result of the awareness (consciousness) of this information.

By emphasising patterns in training, the player's awareness and game sense can be improved. In turn, this will optimise his creativity in the game by increasing the number of playing options that the player recognises.

Shapes can be applied in various ways to train patterns. Most obviously, they can be used in passing games keeping a team shape in a triangle, square or diamond shape and so on. The shape of the practice pitch can also be varied; this will help players to recognise and utilise restricted play areas to pass the ball in real game situations.

The use of coloured bibs is also a great aid to train patterns. The combination of colours and patterns can be used to increase the complexity during the training. Similarly, the use of different shapes on a bib (triangle, circle, square) can aid the development of the player by creating a complicated set of circumstances in training.

Training patterns this way will make the circumstances in a match relatively simple in comparison and increase the player's game sense.

Vision in Goalkeeping

The goalkeeper has an extremely important role in the team. A good goalkeeper 'reads the game well'. He has a good positional sense, not only of himself but also of the other players. Just like field players, the better goalkeeper is able to react to a new set of circumstances by applying learned patterns to create new ones. He is able to anticipate and react. He is more decisive as a result. This is important in all aspects of the goalkeeper's game, including set pieces. It is also important in the prevention of injuries as he is much more likely to avoid clumsy and badly timed challenges.

In some ways it can be argued that reading the game is even more important for goalkeepers, as poor positioning will be more noticeable and will much more often result in a goal. He needs to be in line with play, needs to narrow the angle and needs to be aware of the position of opponents who may also pose a danger, for example by drawing away defenders or by being ready to receive the ball, being ready to receive crosses.

Conclusion

The nervous system receives an enormous amount of stimuli continuously. The information is processed and the nervous system programs reactions. Mostly these reactions involve movements. By training reactions to certain stimuli the brain can learn patterns and create new patterns or maps for future use. This principle can be applied to soccer (team sports) training. As a large part of the information is visual, visual aids can be used for training to develop better 'vision of the game'. We hope that we have given the reader an insight behind the anatomical and physiological processes that support the training methods described in the second part of the book.

PART 2

FOOTBALL EXERCISES
PRACTICAL APPROACH

Introduction

I recently taught my daughter the basic mechanics of driving, before putting her in the hands of a driving instructor. The first few times behind the wheel, her main aim was not to hit anything. She continually looked straight ahead and there was little or no movement from the eyes or head. I took her out daily, over a period of three weeks, and her skill and confidence quickly improved. Her focus expanded and, instead of just looking straight ahead, she began to use the side and rear view mirrors. She became aware of the entire driving situation and started to make her own decisions, instead of relying on me to make them for her. By the time she was ready for the driving instructor, handling a car had almost become second nature. She was able to deal with much more information, drive at greater speed and focus on what was important and delete what was unimportant.

It is easy to equate learning to drive with playing football. After the first few lessons there is little point driving in an empty car park! Sooner rather than later, the driver has to be put in situations where decisions have to be made and perception becomes an essential part of the learning process. We believe that coaching football is the same and that there must be much less emphasis on the repetitive drilling of movements and more on games where players are constantly moving, making decisions and reacting to outside stimuli (e.g. team mates, opponents etc). Just like driving a car, it is essential that players are put into games where they have to constantly interpret the information around them, as this is the optimum environment in which a team or an individual can learn. It is the competition provided by one's opponent that helps create the constantly changing situations on the field. Players will not become decision-makers if the only experience they get is of drills and practices devoid of decision-making opportunities!

The coach's role must be to provide the players with the structure and objectives of the exercise and then let them play. By letting the practices run, players are given the opportunity to work things out for themselves. This engages them in 'discovery learning' and forces them to regularly consider their own sensory feedback. If the coach continually steps in, he breaks up the process that leads to players' game understanding and decision-making. A good coach will know when to stop the practice, in order to correct and re-focus the players, and then let them proceed again with their experiential learning. By adopting such unobtrusive strategies, he will force the players to think about the decisions they make and their consequences.

This approach has further been enhanced by a recent Finnish study that looked at secondary school students' decision-making and game-play ability in soccer. The students played three different 3 v 3 games of football, in a 32m x 20m playing area, for 10 minutes. All matches were video recorded and analysed afterwards, using a coded instrument developed for examining the components of game performance, decision-making and skill execution. The players made significantly more tactical decisions (offensive and defensive) than ball skill executions (receives, passes, dribbles, shots, duels and interceptions) during playing time. The highest number of decisions recorded, in a 10-minute game, was 203 and the highest number of ball skill executions was 54. Considering the ball was only in play for a maximum of 73% of playing time, the results reveal that decision-making, in a game situation, is as important as the execution of motor skills. It was perhaps no coincidence that the students with the best game understanding were also superior at skill execution in game play!

The way forward in visual training appears to be training the way visual information is obtained, perceived and then used. Mann and Gorman used a computer analogy where the eyes and visual pathways were considered as the hardware and the perceptual components of performance, particularly the ability to read the game, were considered as the software. If a player's vision is normal, then the focus should always be on developing the software!

In all fast-moving ball games where the situation is changing constantly, a high demand is placed on players' ability to process information from their environment. Unfortunately, just because they look roughly in the right direction does not necessarily mean that they understand what they see. In "Cognition and Reality", Neisser said "We can only see what we know how to look for." We believe it is the coach's job to open the eyes of the players to the possibilities that exist and to help them focus their attention on important cues, which will lead to greater perception and faster decision-making. It is vital that we 'coach' the mind and the cognitive processes, not just technique.

This book concentrates on vision of play and emphasises that football is a sport based on the ability of the player to instantly analyse and make decisions in constantly changing situations. The fact is players must train to a higher level (known as acute overload), so that they are capable of reacting correctly and more quickly to the stimuli received during play. A combination of experience and perception will enable a player to become an expert who not only memorises certain phases of the game but who looks for new solutions to complex situations.

Increasing the speed and accuracy of mental processing must be a vital part of every training session. At the upper level of soccer, everyone is gifted physically - players have similar speed, strength and power - whilst technically there is little difference between professionals who play in the same position. Therefore, why do players who possess similar physical and technical abilities vary so much in their performance? Our research suggests that it is the speed of mental processing that makes the difference, so future development must focus on training vision and mind speed.

We believe that the exercises we have devised - involving peripheral vision, tag games, random agility, balance, colour, shape and the use of reactor bibs and head-up hats - will help develop players' perception and mental processing and so enable them to become quicker and more skilled decision-makers. Clearly, visual search is a crucial part of decision-making and we feel that the following games and exercises will do a great deal to improve visual search strategies.

Peripheral vision, perception and movement - staying with the ball

Our introductory sessions will encourage players to stay with the ball. This will mean having a ball each and running with it, continually looking for space. As players start to use the space more effectively, a greater emphasis will then be placed on feints, dummies, cuts and turns. Players should then work at a fast pace and perform the skills and techniques as quickly as possible. "If you are going to make a mistake, make a fast mistake."

The following technical and tactical qualities should be focused on:

1)   Running with the head up. Encourage players to scan the field in between touches. Use peripheral vision to be aware of other players and the opening and closing of space.

2)   Close control. Players should use both feet and keep the ball within a stride. It is important that control is not lost and that the ball does not strike other players.

3)   Change of direction. The ability to beat opponents by quick changes of direction is essential.

4)   Bent knees. The knees must be bent so that players can accelerate, stop, start and change direction, whilst one arm should be up to act as an antenna.

5)   Change of pace. Use a change of tempo to practise getting past opponents.

Exercise 1 〉〉〉〉〉

Equipment: 6 cones, footballs and a set of bibs

Number of players: 12 to 16

Dimensions: 2 x 15m x 15m grid

The Game:

- Two 15m grids are set up as in the diagram.

- The players are divided into two equal groups, with one group wearing bibs.

- The players have a ball each and dribble freely in their grid - twisting, turning and being creative.

- As players become more proficient, the coach can introduce new situations, but must make sure the basics have been covered first.

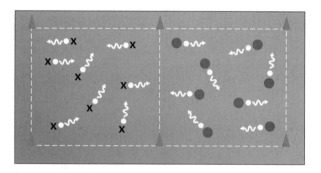

Progression One

- On the coach's signal, the players work the ball as fast as possible.
- When players see space, they sprint into it with the ball.
- When players see space, they perform a trick and then sprint into it with the ball.
- When the coach shouts 'change', the players leave their ball, take someone else's and continue dribbling.
- When the coach shouts 'change', the players leave their ball, change grids and continue dribbling with someone else's ball.

Progression Two

- Players dribble towards each other, drop their left shoulder and move around to the right.
- Players dribble towards each other, drop their right shoulder and move around to the left.
- Players dribble towards each other, stop in front of each other, pull the ball back and dribble away at speed in another direction.
- Players dribble towards each other, stop their ball, take their partner's and dribble away in another direction.

Progression Three

- The middle line of the grid is opened up and players work freely in either grid, still with a ball each.

- The middle line of the grid is replaced and all the players work in one 15m x 15m grid. With space more restricted, tighter control and better peripheral vision are now required.

Progression Four

- One player wears a bib and acts as leader.

- He dribbles freely around the area finding space.

- Every time he stops his ball, the other players must also stop.

Exercise 2 〉〉〉〉〉

Equipment: 6 cones, footballs and a set of bibs

Number of players: 12 to 16

Dimensions: 2 x 15m x 15m grid

The Game:

- Two 15-metre grids are set up as in the diagram.

- All the Os have a ball each and can dribble anywhere they like in their grid.

- Xs enter Os' grid and try to win a ball and dribble it back to their own grid.

- If an O loses his ball, he must chase back and try to win the ball back.

- Work for three minutes and then allow Xs to start with the ball.

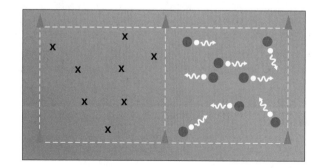

Exercise 3

The Game:

- 'Playing in the future'

- The players have a ball each and dribble freely in the grid.

- As they dribble, players must call out what they are going to do BEFORE carrying out the action e.g. "attacking space", "outside cut", "Cruyff turn", "step over", "speeding up", "drag back", "dribbling with left foot" and so on.

- This will make players think ahead and be more spatially aware.

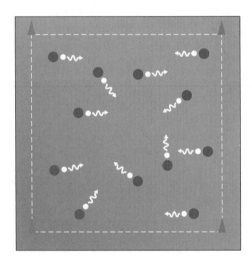

Progression One

- To improve peripheral vision players call out the names of players who come into their visual field e.g. "Tony on my right", "Chris in front of me", "Bill on my left", "Joe behind me on my right" and so on.

Progression Two

- Combine the two activities so that players call out what action they are going to do before carrying it out and shout the names of the players in their visual field.

Exercise 4

The Game:

- Three 10-metre grids are set up, as in the diagram.

- The players are divided into three equal groups, with a maximum of six players per grid.

- The players have a ball each and dribble freely in their grid, twisting, turning and being creative.

- Once a pattern has been established, take out one ball.

- Those with the footballs carry on dribbling, but also play wall passes with the spare player.

- It is essential that those with the footballs are aware of other players and don't pass to the spare man at the same time as someone else!

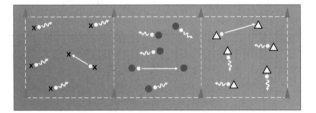

Variation

- As well as playing wall passes, those with the footballs can perform take-overs or drag backs with the spare player.

- However, players must communicate so each knows what action is about to take place.

- The spare player will now be changing regularly.

Progression

- Gradually reduce the number of footballs until there are only two in the grid.

- Those with the footballs can dribble, perform tricks etc as well as carry out different actions with the spare players.

- The players must always know where both footballs are.

Exercise 5

The Game:

- Players work in pairs and each pair has a ball.

- One player stands behind the other.

- The player in front dribbles his ball and continually changes direction and pace.

- The player behind follows his movements as closely as possible.

- The roles should be changed frequently.

Progression

- Two players work side by side, about three metres apart and each with a football.

- One player dribbles his ball and changes pace and direction continuously.

- His partner must keep an eye on him and follow his movements as closely as possible.

- This progression is much more difficult as players have to divide their vision between two directions.

- They have to be aware of their ball moving forwards and also the direction of the partner as he dribbles his ball on one side.

Exercise 6

The Game:

- A 20-metre square is marked out with four cones.

- Five players line up on each side of the square.

- At a signal from the coach, the players start at the same time and sprint across the square and back 10 times.

- The players move as quickly as possible and sprint into space whenever they see it.

- The coach can specify what type of turn he wants at each end e.g. turn on right foot, turn on left foot, jump and turn 180 degrees, touch down with right or left hand etc.

- Which player or line can complete the course first?

- As well as vision training, this can also be used as a fitness exercise.

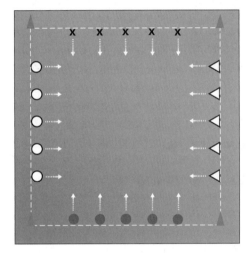

Variation

- As above, but players use the centre circle.

Progression One

- Players sprint backward across the grid 10 times. This will make vision training much harder, as players will have to turn their heads.

Progression Two

- Players have a ball each and dribble across the square and back 10 times. Encourage them to perform a trick in the middle.

Peripheral vision, perception and movement – passing

Passing and receiving are interrelated skills and therefore should be practised together. They are essential for effective teamwork and maintaining possession of the ball. During a game, players are constantly moving, so space continuously opens and closes. It is vital that players recognise this and stay with the ball, waiting for the best moment to pass. We should also be aware that peripheral vision is most sensitive to movement, then to colour and shape. It is vital, therefore, that if a player is to develop his peripheral vision, he must be continually put into training games where teammates and opponents are always on the move. Games where two footballs are used should also be set up, so that players have to watch the line of the other ball whilst passing their own.

Exercise 7

The Game:

- Two players, each with a ball, dribble in a parallel line, about eight metres apart.
- One of them passes his ball across to his partner at a moment of his choosing.
- The partner watches the other player and, at the same time, if possible, passes his ball.
- Players take it in turns to initiate the first pass.

Exercise 8

The Game:

- Two players, one with a ball, run side by side about five metres apart.
- The player without the ball sometimes runs behind, sometimes parallel and sometimes in front of the player with the ball.
- The player without the ball could call for it in any one of these positions, so the player with the ball must use his peripheral vision to keep an eye on his partner, and pass the ball to the correct position when asked.
- The roles should be changed continuously.

Exercise 9

The Game:

- Three players stand in a triangle about seven metres apart. Each player has a ball.
- They start off with the ball in the hand and volley pass to each other simultaneously.
- They pass to the left or right, according to the instructions of the coach.
- When a rhythm has been established, the ball is placed on the ground and passed with the inside of the foot.
- At any one time, the players are forced not only to look at the player they have passed to, but also at the ball coming towards them.
- Players should try to use one-touch passing whenever possible.
- One player should always give the order to start.

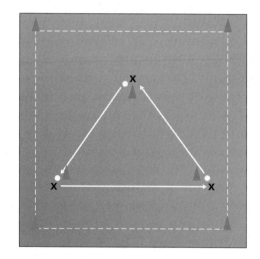

Exercise 10 〉〉〉〉〉

The Game:

- Players take up positions in three corners of a square. The fourth corner is left free. X1 has a ball.

- X1 passes to X2, then sprints for the free corner.

- X2 passes to X3 and sprints for the free corner.

- The process is continuous. Encourage players to pass first time.

- Before receiving the ball, players should use their peripheral vision in order to identify the free corner.

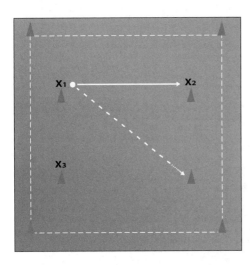

Equipment: 4 cones, 2 footballs
Number of players: 8 to 10
Dimensions: 12m x 12m grid

The Game:

- Players form a tight circle, inside a 12-metre square.

- They start off with one ball and pass, one touch, with the inside of the foot.

- When a rhythm has been established, a second ball is added and both have to be passed without being gathered.

- The aim is to prevent both balls hitting or meeting at any one player.

- The player passing the ball must therefore keep an eye on the path of the other ball, so that they do not collide.

- As players become more efficient, make the circle smaller.

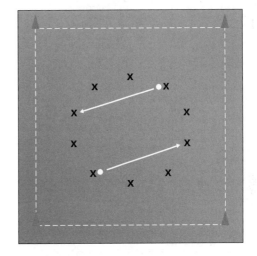

Progression

- For more advanced players, a defender can now be introduced.

- Start off one-touch passing, with one ball, but quickly add another if players can cope.

- The players not only have to watch the ball they are passing and the path of the second ball, they also have to be aware of the position of the defender.

Exercise 12 》》》》》

Equipment: 4 cones, 2 footballs

Number of players: 8 to 10

Dimensions: 12m x 12m grid

The Game:

- Players form a tight circle inside a 12-metre square.

- They start off with one ball and pass it with the inside of the foot.

- After passing the ball, the player sprints to a gap in the circle. He **cannot** follow his pass.

- The players on the outside have to quickly adjust their position, in order to keep the circle balanced.

- When a rhythm has been established, a second ball is introduced and this has to be passed one- or two-touch.

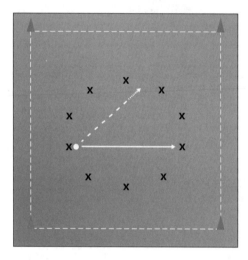

Progression

- For more advanced players, a defender is now added.

- Start off with one ball and allow one- or two-touch passing.

- Players have to readjust quickly on the outside, so that the circle is always balanced.

- Once players can cope with one ball, quickly add a second.

- Players now have to be aware of the ball they are passing, the spare ball, gaps in the circle and the defender.

- This exercise will not only improve peripheral vision, but also the ability to analyse situations quickly, and will emphasise the importance of a good first touch.

Exercise 13 》》》》》

Equipment: 4 cones, 2 footballs

Number of players: 5

Dimensions: 12m x 12m grid

The Game:

- Five players take up random positions in a 12-metre square and stand still.

- They start off with one ball and pass it with the inside of the foot.

- When a rhythm has been established, introduce a second ball.

- The aim is to prevent both balls colliding or ending up at the same player.

- With so few players, this is a very difficult practice.

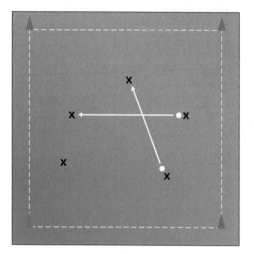

Progression

- For more advanced players, allow them to move anywhere in the square.

- The player passing the ball must therefore keep an eye on the path of the other ball and the movement of the players.

Exercise 14 〉〉〉〉

Equipment: 4 cones, 3 footballs

Number of players: 6

Dimensions: 12m x 12m grid

The Game:

- The players are in a team of six and work in a 12-metre square.

- A player stands in each corner; three of these players have a ball.

- The fourth player does not have a ball and acts as the first receiver.

- None of the corner players can move more than two metres in any direction from their corner.

- The two players in the square are designated attacker (O1) and defender (O2).

- O1 can move anywhere he likes in the square and collect a pass from any of the players with a ball.

- On receiving the ball O1 moves and dribbles to get away from O2 and then passes to the corner player without a ball.

- Once successful, he moves around the square, collects another pass from one of the corners and delivers it to the player without a ball.

- The drill continues for two minutes and then the middle pair is replaced.

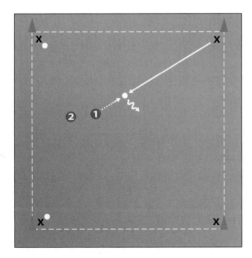

Progression

- The players on the outside dribble slowly around the square, making sure that each side is always covered.

- O1 moves where he likes in the square and collects a pass from any player with a ball.

- On receiving the ball, O1 feints and dribbles to get away from O2 and then passes to the spare player without a ball.

- Once successful, he moves around the square, collects another pass from one of the outside players and delivers it to the player without a ball.

- This task is much more difficult as there is now constant movement and the attacking player has to continually scan the field in order to find the spare player.

Exercise 15 〉〉〉〉

Equipment: 4 cones, 1 football

Number of players: 4

Dimensions: 5m x 5m grid

The Game:

- Three players stand on three sides of a 5-metre square.

- The fourth player, O, stands in the middle of the square.

- The aim of the practice is to try to hit the legs of the player on the inside with the ball.

- The player on the inside tries to avoid being hit by running, jumping, twisting and dodging.

- The outside players must be alert and move around the square in order to prevent the ball rolling away.

- They should try to anticipate where the ball will go if it misses the inside player.

- Make the game competitive and allow each player a turn in the middle.

- Only provide one ball. The outside players must then attempt to read where the ball will go, since any lack of anticipation will cost time if the ball rolls away.

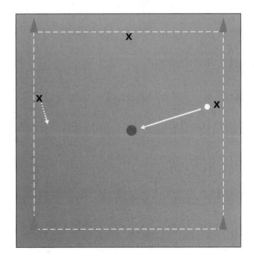

Progression

- Play 3 v 1.

- The attacking players may move around the outside of the grid but not enter it.

Exercise 16 ⟩⟩⟩⟩⟩

Equipment: 4 cones, 2 footballs

Number of players: 8 to 10

Dimensions: 15m x 15m grid

The Game:

- Four to six players occupy the middle of a 15-metre square.

- One more player stands on each side of the square.

- The players in the middle randomly pass a ball amongst themselves.

- Every third or fourth pass must be played to an outside player, but before doing this the middle player must call out the name of the player he is going to pass to.

- The outside player has two touches to return the ball, but NOT to the player who passed to him.

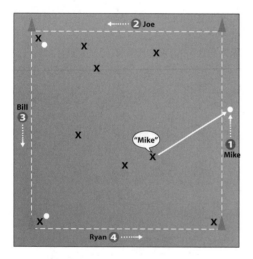

Variation

- When a rhythm has been established, introduce a second ball.

Progression

- For more advanced players, the outside players now jog slowly around the square, making sure that each side is covered at all times.

- The inside players still have to call out who they are going to pass to before receiving the ball.

- This will require far greater visual awareness by all players, particularly if a second ball is involved.

Exercise 17 ≫≫≫≫

Equipment: 10 cones, 4 footballs and a set of bibs

Number of players: 12+

Dimensions: 4 x 20m x 8m grids

The Game:

- The field is divided into four equal zones.

- Each team has two zones, which do not border on each other.

- Each team has a ball and attempts to pass through the other team's zones.

- A team may pass within its own zone, until a gap appears.

- This is a free-flowing game and the opposition players must not attempt to disrupt the passes as the ball travels through their zone.

- When players can cope with one ball, add another.

- Players should change zones regularly so that all players get a chance to work in the more challenging middle zones.

Variation

- Players can change zones but they cannot cross their opponent's zone.

- Instead, they have to go around the outside.

- There must always be an equal number of players in each zone.

Progression One

- Players can perform take-overs and drag backs in their opponent's middle zone.

- This will require good communication, both verbal and visual, and an awareness of the opponent's position within the zone.

Progression Two

- The game now becomes competitive.

- Using one ball, teams try to pass through the opponent's zone and back again, without the opposition touching the ball. Every time the team is successful, they score a point.

Progression Three

- One player from the defending team may enter the attacking zone, thereby creating a 4 v 1 situation. If the ball is moved out of the attacking zone, the defender must return to his original zone.

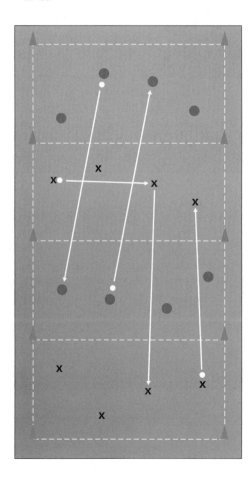

Equipment: 12 cones, 4 footballs and 2 sets of bibs

Number of players: 14

Dimensions: 6 x 8m x 8m grids

Equipment: 6 cones, 4 footballs and bibs

Number of players: 12

Dimensions: 2 x 15m x 30m grids

The Game:

- The field is divided into six equal squares.

- There is one player from each team in each square.

- There are two additional players who may work in any of the squares.

- Each team has two footballs and they pass amongst themselves, making sure that both footballs do not end up at the same player.

- Both teams may use the spare players.

The Game:

- The field is divided into two equal zones, with three players from each team in each zone and two footballs per team.

- Players must remain in their half of the field.

- The two teams pass through each other but are not against each other.

- Players must play with their heads up and be aware of teammates' and opponents' positions on the field.

- Players pass, dribble, perform take-overs etc in their own grid, until eye contact is made with a player in the other grid. The ball is then passed across.

- It is vital that players are constantly scanning the field and have the ability to look away from the ball as well as at it.

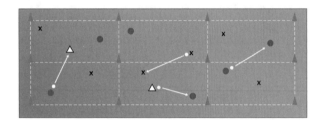

Progression One

- To encourage more movement and greater awareness, allow players to change zones.

- However, there must always be a player in each zone, so as one moves in another must move out.

Progression Two

- Once a rhythm has been established, take out three footballs.

- The game now becomes competitive, with each team trying to keep possession of the ball.

- The two extra players always play for the team in possession and can move anywhere in the field.

- For more experienced players, add a second ball. Can one team keep possession of both footballs?

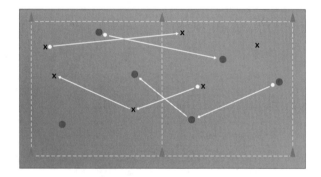

Progression

- Introduce two more teams to the same area and have the four teams play through each other.

- This will require even greater awareness and peripheral vision from all players and a much bigger effort will be required to create space.

Exercise 20 »»»

Equipment: 8 cones, 2 footballs and a set of bibs

Number of players: 8 to 12

Dimensions: 3 x 20m x 20m grids

The Game:

- The field is divided into three zones, two end zones and one neutral zone, with five players in each end zone and the neutral zone free.

- Players pass and move in their own zone until eye contact is made with a player in the other zone or a call is made. A pass is then made to that player.

- Balls will be constantly changing zones, so players will not only need to be visually aware in their own zone, they will also need to be aware of when a pass is on from the other zone.

- Players must **always** have their heads up and be constantly looking around, observing all the options in both zones.

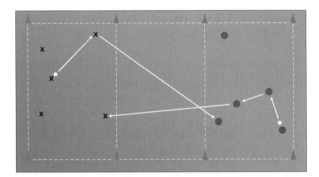

Progression One

- Once a pattern has been established, allow players to dribble across the zones, as well as perform take-overs and drag backs in the neutral zone, with players from the other zone.

- This will require excellent verbal and visual communication.

- There must always be a balance of players and footballs in each end zone.

Progression Two

- A player from the other end zone makes a run into the neutral zone.

- The player with the ball must see this and pass to the player making the run.

- The receiver attempts to take the ball sideways on and dribble back to his own zone.

- If a player makes a run into the neutral zone and doesn't receive a pass, then he must return immediately to his own zone.

Progression Three

- Introduce a defender in each end zone, making two 4 v 1 situations.

- Only one ball will now be required.

Exercise 21 »»»

Equipment: 4 cones, 1 football

Number of players: 5

Dimensions: 30m x 20m grid

The Game:

- Five players are placed in a 30m x 20m grid. Each player is numbered from 1 to 5.

- Players randomly pass one ball amongst themselves.

- After several passes, X1 makes a run outside the grid.

- Whoever has the ball should see the run and pass to X1.

- If players are thinking ahead, as X1 is about to receive the ball, another player (X3 in this case) should move to support X1.

- The game now continues and after several passes, X2 makes a run outside the grid.

- Once again, whoever has the ball should see the run and pass to X2.

- The process continues with players running outside the grid in sequence.

- Once a player has made his run outside the grid, the coach should count how many passes are made inside the grid before someone sees the outside player.

- This will give an indication of who has good peripheral vision and who hasn't.

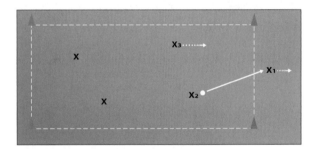

Variation

- Instead of moving in sequence, allow players to randomly sprint outside the grid.

Progression

- Allow another group to work inside the same grid.

- The extra players will limit space and make peripheral vision much more difficult.

Exercise 22 ⟩⟩⟩⟩⟩

Equipment: 6 cones, 2 footballs, 4 goals and bibs

Number of players: 16

Dimensions: 2 x 35m x 35m grids

The Game:

- The field is divided into two grids, each 35m x 35m.

- Teams play 4 v 4 in each grid, with the attacking teams trying to maintain possession of the ball.

- At any stage of the game, players can change places with a partner from the other grid. However, there must always be a balance in both grids.

- Players will need to focus on the ball and movements made by teammates and opponents in their grid.

- At the same time, good peripheral vision will be required, in order to spot any movements made by teammates in the other grid.

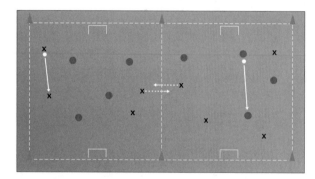

Progression

- Each team attacks and defends a small-sided goal. Goals only count if the ball hits the net off the ground.

- As before, players can change places with a partner from the other grid.

- Whilst completing the switch, players will have to quickly analyse the play, to see how it is developing in the new game.

Exercise 23 ⟩⟩⟩⟩⟩

Equipment: 5 cones and a ball

Number of players: 5

Dimensions: 10m x 10m grid

The Game:

- A 10-metre square is marked out with four cones. A fifth cone is placed in the middle of the square.

- Each player is given a number from 1 to 5.

- The players randomly pass amongst themselves, being careful to avoid the middle cone.

- However, when the coach shouts out "1", number 1 becomes a defender and tries to protect the middle cone from the other four players.

- After a minute, the coach shouts 'change' and the players return to passing amongst themselves.

- When the coach shouts out "2", number 2 becomes the defender and tries to protect the middle cone from the other four players.

- This process continues until all five players have experienced the role of defender.

- Which defender had the least number of strikes against the target?

- This exercise will improve vision and decision-making since players will have to be aware of other attackers, the defender, the ball and the middle cone.

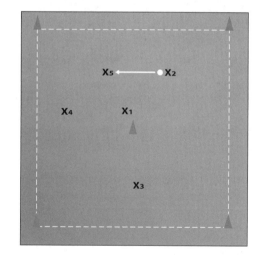

Exercise 24 》》》》

Equipment: 4 cones, 2 footballs and a set of bibs

Number of players: 12

Dimensions: 30m x 25m grid

The Game:

- The players are divided into two teams, with one team wearing bibs.

- Team X starts with the two footballs and tries to keep possession of both.

- If O's win the ball, they also attempt to keep possession.

- Which team is more successful at keeping possession of both footballs?

- After four minutes, allow O's to start with the footballs.

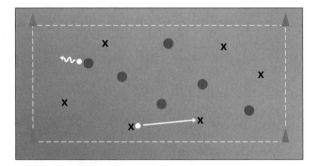

Progression

- Team X starts with two footballs and attempts to keep possession of both.

- If an O wins the ball, he dribbles it to the outside of the grid and leaves it.

- X's have to sprint out to retrieve it and dribble it back into the grid.

- X's must know where both footballs are at all times.

- How many times did an X have to sprint outside the grid to retrieve a ball?

- Change roles after four minutes.

Peripheral vision, movement and one-touch play

There are many times during a game when players, before and after receiving the ball, need to look around and see what is happening on the pitch. In order to keep track of the ball at the same time, players need to use their peripheral vision. One of the best ways to improve this is by playing 'one-touch' football but this requires balance, awareness, anticipation and correct body positioning. Therefore, until players have a high level of technical and tactical ability, one-touch soccer should not be introduced.

Exercise 25 »»»»

Equipment: 4 cones, footballs

Number of players: groups of 6

Dimensions: half a pitch

The Game:

- Players are divided into groups of six, with one ball per group.

- Several groups work together on half a pitch.

- The players pass and move, but all one-touch.

- As soon as players can manage one ball, add a second.

- This is a very difficult exercise, as players have to think about several things at the same time, including finding space and timing their runs. Players have no choice but to concentrate!

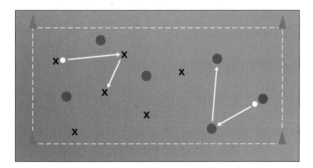

Progression One

- Gradually reduce the space, so players are working on quarter of a pitch and eventually the penalty area.

Progression Two

- Introduce a defender and create a 5 v 1 situation.

- It is still one-touch passing and if not successful at the start, make the defender passive.

- As before, begin on half a pitch and gradually reduce the size of the area.

Exercise 26 »»»»

Equipment: 4 cones, 2 footballs and a set of bibs

Number of players: 14

Dimensions: 60m x 40m grid

The Game:

- A 60m by 40m grid is marked out with four cones.

- The players are divided into two groups of seven, with one group wearing bibs.

- There is one ball per group.

- The two groups pass amongst themselves but do so in the following sequence: one-touch, two-touch, one-touch, two-touch and so on.

- When a rhythm has been established, a game of 'keep ball' is now set up and the attacking team tries to keep possession and score a point by completing eight successive passes.

- However, the ball still has to be passed in the above sequence.

- This is a difficult game and calls for concentration, awareness, quick support and focused and peripheral vision.

- This game should not be attempted by inexperienced players.

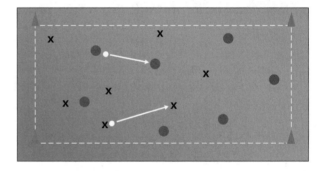

Progression

- Both teams play 'keep ball' and try to play as many one-touch passes as possible.

- Which team can reach 25 one-touch passes first?

Exercise 27 〉〉〉〉〉

Equipment: 2 goals, 8 cones and footballs

Number of players: 14

Dimensions: 60m x 40m grid

The Game:

- A 60m x 40m grid is divided into three equal parts, with a goal placed on each end line.

- The teams play normal football, apart from the following conditions.

- The team in possession is only allowed three-touch play in each end zone and one-touch play in the central zone.

- If there are no goalkeepers, use a one-touch finish to score.

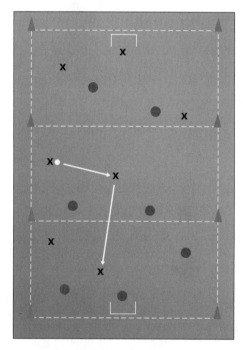

Progression One

- Players are limited to three-touch play in the central zone and one-touch play in the end zones.

- Still use a one-touch finish to score.

Progression Two

- Players are restricted to two touches in **all** zones, when receiving on the ground.

- However, they may have multiple touches when receiving a ball in the air.

Exercise 28 〉〉〉〉〉

Equipment: 20 cones, 6 footballs and 6 bibs

Number of players: 12

Dimensions: 12 x 8m grids

The Game:

- 12 x 8 metre grids are marked out with cones.

- The players are split into pairs, with one player wearing a bib.

- Players start off running and must never be in the same grid as their partner.

- When a rhythm has been established, players sprint to one grid, jog to the next, sprint to the next and so on.

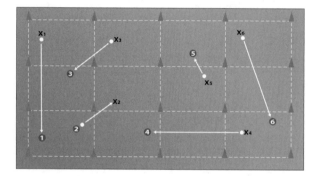

Progression One

- Each pair now has a ball.

- Players pass to their partners, who must always be in a different grid.

- After passing, players sprint to another grid.

Progression Two

- X's have a ball each and play one/two's with O's.

- O's must always be in a different grid to X's.

- After passing, both players sprint into other grids.

- Change roles after two minutes.

Tag Games

During a game, players have to run without the ball for much of it and move into good supporting positions. Often attackers have to run fast over a variety of distances, to get rid of players marking them and to create openings for teammates at the same time. In tag games, the player being chased is performing the role of the attacker. He tries to get away from his marking defender by continually changing direction and pace. The chaser, on the other hand, takes the role of the defender and tries to get as close as possible to the attacker. Tag games (with or without a ball) require feints and dummies, anticipation, agility, peripheral and focused vision, visual scanning speed, change of pace and quick reflexes. They are good fun, create a relaxed atmosphere and are ideal for vision training.

Recently, The Australian Institute of Sport has proposed a new definition of agility: "a rapid whole-body movement with change of velocity or direction in response to a stimulus". We know that agility is connected to trainable physical qualities such as strength and power and cognitive components such as visual scanning techniques, visual scanning speed, anticipation and perception. Since sports such as football often involve repeated short sprints with changes of direction, it seems essential that we provide training that mimics this demand.

In the past, much of the training for agility has involved players running set patterns around stationary objects such as cones or poles. However, these zig-zag runs are pre-planned and do not involve a reaction to a stimulus and so will simply develop change of direction speed rather than agility, as proposed by the Australian Institute. The trigger in a game is nearly always brought about by another player's movement, general movement of play or the ball. This creates significant uncertainty of time and space since players have to respond to the sensory stimuli around them. Tag games provide an open skilled environment in which movements cannot be rehearsed or pre-planned. We believe these games will increase specificity and help promote appropriate visual search strategies and rapid decision-making under pressure. Later in the book, we have included exercises that will put players under even greater pressure by combining tag games with dynamic vision and single leg plyometric exercises.

Exercise 29 〉〉〉〉〉

The Game:

- An area is marked out with four cones and any number of players are scattered within it.
- One player is chosen as catcher and wears a bib.
- His task is to count how many players he can catch within 30 seconds.
- Players touched still carry on in the game.

Variation

- Several players, wearing bibs, are given the role of chasers.
- After one minute, the total for the chasers is added up.
- Which group can catch the most players?
- This makes the game more lively, forces players to move more often and puts much greater emphasis on peripheral and focal vision.

Exercise 30 〉〉〉〉〉

The Game:

- An area is marked out with four cones and any number of pairs are scattered within it.
- Each player in the pair is designated 1 or 2.
- If the coach shouts out "1", 1 chases 2.
- If caught, 2 must perform two press-ups (two squats, two lunges etc) before he can chase 1.
- If 2 catches 1, 1 has to perform two press-ups before he can chase 2.
- This is a very strenuous exercise, so players should only work for 30 seconds before being given a minute's active rest.

Exercise 31 ⟫⟫⟫

The Game:

- An area is marked out with four cones and any number of players are scattered within it.

- Two players are chosen as catchers and wear bibs.

- The players can get rid of their catcher by taking refuge.

- This can take the form of hopping on the spot, sitting down or squatting and the chaser cannot touch them in the refuge position.

- Players can only use the refuge once and may only stay in there for five seconds.

Exercise 32 ⟫⟫⟫

The Game:

- An area is marked out with four cones and any number of trios are scattered within it.

- Each player in the trio is designated 1, 2 or 3.

- If the coach shouts out "2", 2 chases 3.

- Whilst this is happening, 1 should keep as far away from the action as possible.

- If the coach shouts out "3", 3 chases 1 and if he shouts out "1", 1 chases 2.

- The coach must change the numbers every 10 to 15 seconds and NOT work in a set pattern.

- This is a very strenuous exercise and after two minutes players must be allowed one minute's active recovery.

Variation One

- As above, but each player dribbles a ball.

Variation Two

- 1 chases 2 until he catches him, 2 then chases 3 until he catches him and 3 chases 1 until he catches him.

Exercise 33 ⟫⟫⟫

The Game:

- An area is marked out with four cones and players are divided into groups of four.

- Each player in the group is designated 1, 2, 3 or 4.

- 1 chases 2, 2 chases 3, 3 chases 4 and 4 chases 1.

- If caught, a player has to run out of the area and back before he can rejoin the game.

- This is a great game for vision, as players have to be aware of the player they are chasing, the player chasing them, and the rest of the players moving in the area.

Variation

- As before, but each player dribbles a ball.

Exercise 34 ⟫⟫⟫

The Game:

- An area is marked out with four cones and any number of players are scattered within it.

- Two of them are chosen as catchers and wear bibs.

- The catchers try to touch as many players as possible in 30 seconds.

- Any player touched by a catcher must go into a squatting position.

- The coach counts how many squatters there are after 30 seconds and new chasers are then chosen.

Exercise 35 ⟫⟫⟫

The Game:

- An area is marked out with four cones and any number of players are scattered within it.

- Five players are chosen as catchers and each has a ball.

- The catchers must bounce the ball one-handed.

- When they come within striking distance, they head the ball out of their hand at a moving player.

- Each chaser counts how many successful hits he gets in two minutes.

Variation

- The players are divided into two teams, with one team in bibs and designated as chasers.

- The chasers pass and move two balls by hand.

- When they are close enough, they head the ball out of their own hands, or throw it for a teammate to head direct, at a player on the run.

- One point is awarded for each hit.

- After three minutes, the two groups change roles.

Exercise 36 〉〉〉〉〉

The Game:

- A 20-metre square is marked out with four cones.

- Six players have a ball each and two carry bibs.

- All the players dribble their footballs.

- The two chasers try to touch the other players or their footballs.

- If a player being pursued is caught, he changes roles with the pursuer.

Exercise 37 〉〉〉〉〉

The Game:

- A 20-metre square is marked out with four cones.

- Ten players have a ball each and dribble them within the square.

- Five other players carry a ball in their hands.

- They try to hit the balls being dribbled.

- The other players shield the balls and use feints and dummies to prevent this.

- The chasers count how many balls they hit in three minutes.

Somatosensory, visual and vestibular systems involved in maintaining balance

Balance is the integral part of movement and without it, the player is continually wasting energy. Therefore, once players have become proficient at the following single- and double-leg squatting exercises, it is essential to put them into dynamic movements which will integrate several of the body systems involved in maintaining balance. These will include the somatosensory system, which provides information from the vibration receptors in the skin and proprioceptors in the muscles, joints and ligaments; the visual system which provides information about the relationship of the head and eyes to surrounding objects and is primarily used when the support surface is unstable; and the vestibular system, located in the inner ear, which gives information about head movements relative to gravity.

Most of the exercises will be single-leg, since sports such as football are never played on two feet. Instead, the player continuously moves from one foot to the other, so it is vital that single-leg strength exercises work in conjunction with the visual, vestibular and somatosensory systems, to form the basis of most balance work. The aim of all the balancing activities will be to combine the three systems whilst maintaining body control.

Photo 2

The body weight squat, as shown in Photo 1, can be used as a lead-in to the other squatting exercises, so proper technique is important. Start with the hands at shoulder height and the fingers to the side of the head. The feet are approximately shoulder width apart, slightly turned out at about 10 to 15 degrees and flat on the floor. The chest should be open and the upper and lower back slightly arched (i.e. in the neutral position). The head must stay upright at all times.

When descending into the squat, as shown in Photo 2, sit back and place the body weight on the heels (not on the balls of the feet as this creates a forward lean). The player bends at the knees and hips, until the thighs are parallel to the floor. During the descent, the knees should stay over the toes and not in front. The player then returns to the starting position. The back and head should stay as upright as possible - the spine maintaining the neutral position - whilst the heels drive into the floor.

Photo 1

Photo 3

Instability is now added to the front squat. The player stands on a balance board or an inflatable stability disc and performs the same drill as the body weight squat above. The instability of the board provides additional proprioceptive stress to the lower body and develops balance at the same time. It also forces the player to concentrate on technique and weight distribution. If boards are not available, use two tennis balls instead. See Photo 3.

If players are unable to carry out this exercise, they should take their arms to the side in order to aid balance.

The single-leg squat requires the use of one leg, without any help to balance from the opposite leg. The pelvic muscles act as stabilisers, as long as the opposite leg does not touch the ground. The player attempts to squat on one leg, to a position where the thigh is parallel to the floor. The weight must be kept on the heel and the knee should not move beyond the big toe. This is a very difficult exercise and most players feel unsteady the first few times and find it difficult to reach the parallel position. For better-conditioned players, it is possible to carry out this exercise on a balance board or an inflated stability disc. See Photos 4 and 5.

Photo 4

Photo 6

Photo 5

Photo 7

The player stands with feet shoulder width apart and hands clasped behind the head. He squats down to a parallel position and jumps as high as possible, then put the feet in dorsiflexion (ie. toes up). He lands on the balls of the feet, lowers his heels and slightly bends the knees to absorb the shock and repeats the sequence. See Photos 6 and 7.

The player stands on one foot, in a one-quarter squat position. He then drops his hips, swings his arms, drives his right leg up and reaches forward to gain distance. He lands on the same foot, continues to hop, while the left leg is held in a stationary position throughout the exercise. The better-conditioned athlete should pull the heel of the jumping leg towards the buttocks during the jump. See Photos 8 and 9.

Photo 8

Photo 9

The Layout:

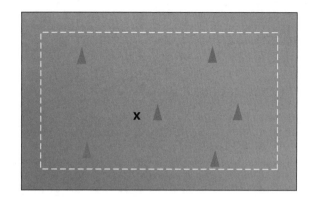

- Six cones, footballs or other markers are set up as in the above diagram.
- Two markers are 1 metre and 4 metres in front of the player, two are 4 metres to his right and left and two are 4 metres behind him on his right and left.

Exercise 38 〉〉〉〉〉

The Game:

- The player stands on one leg and at the same time changes focus quickly from the near marker to the far marker and back to the near marker. Repeat several times.
- He then changes focus to the marker on his left, then to the marker on his right and back to the marker on his left. Repeat several times.
- He changes focus again to the markers behind him, on his left and right and back to the left. Repeat several times.
- Repeat the above on the other leg.
- The second and third exercises are much more difficult as turning the head causes inner ear disturbance, making balance much more difficult.

Progression

- The player balances on one leg, brings his knee to the parallel and places his hands on his hips.
- This raises and narrows the centre of gravity and makes the exercise more difficult.

The player performs the following exercises whilst continually changing focus through the six positions indicated in the layout on the previous page.

Exercise 39 〉〉〉〉〉

- The player performs squats. When competent, the player performs the squat on a balance board, inflated air-ball cushion or tennis balls.

Exercise 40 〉〉〉〉〉

- Hopping forwards and backwards on the left and right legs, as well as both legs together.

Exercise 41 〉〉〉〉〉

- The player hops backwards and forwards on one leg and works a ball with the foot of the other. Keep changing the balance and sensorial legs.

Exercise 42 〉〉〉〉〉

- Hop on the left leg and then the right leg, from side to side.

Exercise 43 〉〉〉〉〉

- Hop backwards and forwards over a ball, whilst changing direction freely.

Exercise 44 〉〉〉〉〉

- The player juggles a ball.

Exercise 45 〉〉〉〉〉

- The player balances a ball on his foot.

Exercise 46 〉〉〉〉〉

- Work in pairs. One player hops backwards and forwards on one leg, whilst his partner serves him a ball to head/ volley back.
- Between volleys or headers, the player moves his visual field through any of the six positions indicated.

Random agility plus vision, hearing and balance

We now need to put the players into a more realistic sport situation, by placing them in an unpredictable environment. They will carry out basic, low-level plyometric drills and perform most of the jumps on single legs. However, there will be some two-footed jumps, in order to reduce the strain on the legs. Each exercise will last no longer than 10 to 15 seconds and in between players will walk, jog or run according to the instructions of the coach.

By allowing players to randomly move around the area, whilst running, jumping, accelerating, decelerating and changing direction, it will enable them to combine dynamic vision and balance training, as they will have to be aware of the field, space and other players. In addition, these functional exercises will force players to move through the vertical, horizontal and rotational planes of movement (sometimes at the same time), which they have to do in a game and are essential for injury prevention.

The following plyometric drills are now put into a random agility format:

- Hopping on both legs forwards, backwards and sideways.

- Single-leg hops forwards.

- Single-leg hops backwards.

- Single-leg hops laterally (sideways, away from the body).

- Single-leg hops medially (sideways, towards the body).

- Single-leg hops diagonally (zigzag). These can be carried out forwards, backwards, laterally and medially.

A greater load can be placed on players' visual, vestibular and somatosensory systems by making them perform the above exercises with a football or light medicine ball held above the head. Without the use of the arms (which provide balance and compensate for rotational forces), the core muscles now have to work much harder. In addition, the centre of gravity is changed, which makes the player land more upright. This takes away some of the forces which occur when decelerating through the hips and ensures that the quadriceps are used for knee flexion.

The following exercises will all involve the low-level plyometric drills as listed above.

Exercise 47 〉〉〉〉〉

Equipment: 4 cones
Number of players: 16
Dimensions: 20m x 20m grid

The Game:

- A 20-metre square is marked out with four cones.

- Sixteen players move randomly around the square.

- Whilst moving, players carry out the low-level plyometric drills, as instructed by the coach.

- In between activities, players walk or jog in order to aid recovery.

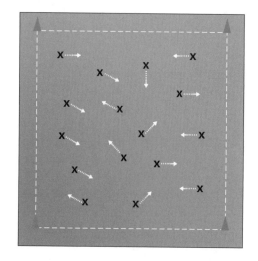

Exercise 48 ⟫⟫⟫

Equipment: 16 cones and 16 footballs

Number of players: 16

Dimensions: 20m x 20m grid

The Game:

- A maximum of 16 players, each with a ball, in a 20-metre square.

- Players start by dribbling, getting in lots of twists and turns with the ball. They must be spatially aware at all times.

- On a signal, the players leave their footballs wherever they are.

- They then sprint around the area and toe-touch as many footballs as possible in 20 seconds.

- It is important that players turn often during this exercise and don't just run in a circle or straight line.

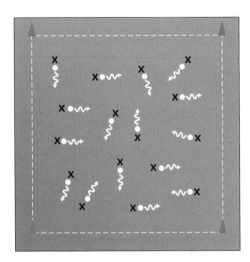

Progression One

- On a signal, the players leave their balls and sprint to the first ball, jog backwards to the second, jockey to the third, shuffle sideways to the fourth and sprint to the fifth.

Progression Two

- On a signal, the players leave their balls and hop to the first ball, hop backwards to the second, hop laterally to the third, hop medially to the fourth and hop diagonally to the fifth.

- The coach will tell players which leg to hop on.

Exercise 49 ⟫⟫⟫

Equipment: 4 cones and 16 footballs

Number of players: 16

Dimensions: 20m x 20m grid

The Game:

- A 20-metre square is marked out with four cones. Eight pairs of players are scattered within it.

- Each pair is designated 1 or 2 and both players carry a football above the head.

- If the coach shouts out "1", 1 chases 2 - and vice versa.

- The players start off running (either forwards or backwards), but when a rhythm has been established they change to any of the low-level plyometric drills, as instructed by the coach.

- Players should only work for 15 seconds at a time as this game is very strenuous.

- In between activities, players walk or jog in order to aid recovery.

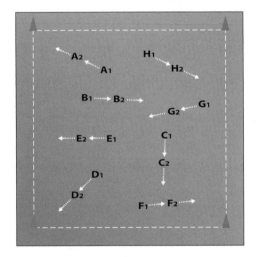

Exercise 50 ⟫⟫⟫

Equipment: 4 cones, 4 footballs and 4 bibs

Number of players: 16

Dimensions: 20m x 20m grid

The Game:

- A 20-metre square is marked out with four cones and 12 players are scattered within it.

- Four more players act as chasers, wear bibs and carry footballs above their heads.

- The four chasers have 30 seconds to catch as many players as possible, by touching them with the ball.

- The players start off running, but when a rhythm has been established, they use any of the low-level plyometric drills, as instructed by the coach.

- The coach could also change the actions several times within the 30 seconds e.g. hop on right leg, hop backwards on left leg, hop with a zig-zag on right leg etc.

- At the end of 30 seconds, the chasers count up how many players they have caught and four different players are then assigned as chasers.

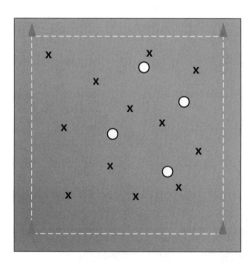

Exercise 51 ⟫⟫⟫

Equipment: 4 cones, 1 football and a set of bibs

Number of players: 12

Dimensions: 20m x 20m grid

The Game:

- A 20-metre square is marked out with four cones.

- The players are divided into two teams of six, with one team in bibs. The game is played like handball and players throw and catch using their hands.

- The opposition can only win the ball through interceptions.

- The players start off moving normally, but quickly change to any of the low-level plyometric drills, as instructed by the coach.

- The coach should change the actions quickly as the game is very tiring e.g. from handball to handball hopping on left leg, handball hopping backwards on right leg and back to normal handball.

- The usual game of handball should always be used as the recovery period and players work on the plyometric drills for 20 seconds and normal handball for 1 minute.

- Once again, this is a functional exercise as the players have to see the field, the opposition and the best passing options, as well as being forced to constantly change body position, direction and centre of gravity.

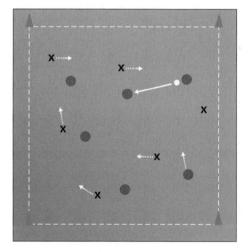

Progression

- One player from each team stands on each end line.

- The aim is to get the ball from one end player and pass to the other, without losing possession to the defending team.

- As before, the players start off moving normally, but quickly change to any of the low-level plyometric drills, as instructed by the coach.

- There must be a minimum of three passes before the ball can be thrown to an end player.

Exercise 52 ⟫⟫⟫⟫⟫

The Game:

- The players are divided into two teams of six, with one team in bibs.

- The teams play 'keep ball' but volley the ball out of their hands for a teammate to catch.

- Players may run with the ball before volleying.

- The opposition can only win the ball through interceptions.

- The players start off running normally but quickly change to any of the low-level plyometric drills, as instructed by the coach.

- The coach should change the actions quickly, as this is an extremely tiring game e.g. volley pass whilst hopping on left leg, then volley pass whilst hopping backwards on right leg and back to volley pass whilst running normally.

- The hopping/volley games should last no longer than 20 seconds, whilst normal running and volley should last a minute each time and be used as the recovery period.

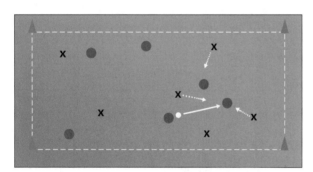

Variation

- As above, except players head the ball out of their own hands to a teammate.

- Once more, allow players to run with the ball and head out of their hands first, before changing to the various hopping exercises plus heading.

- The volleying and heading are both very functional exercises since players have to perform a football skill whilst seeing the field, the opposition and the best passing options, as well being forced to change body position and centre of gravity continually.

Progression

- When receiving a volley or headed pass, players control the ball with any part of their body first before catching the ball.

- This is a very difficult exercise, particularly when operating on one leg, and should only be attempted by more advanced players.

Exercise 53 ⟫⟫⟫⟫⟫

The Game:

- Six players have a football each and are the chasers. The six players on the other team have a bib tucked into the back of their shorts.

- Those with the soccer balls attempt to snatch as many bibs as possible in one minute.

- Those with the bibs attempt to keep them, but may only move by hopping.

- They can change their hopping leg whenever they wish, but must only move on one leg.

- After one minute see how many bibs the chasers have collected.

- Players then change roles.

- Which team has the most bibs?

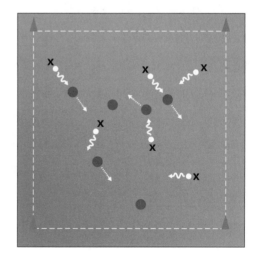

Exercise 54 >>>>>

Equipment: 4 cones and 12 footballs

Number of players: 12

Dimensions: 20m x 20m grid

The Game:

- A 20-metre square is set up, as in the diagram below.

- The players have a ball each and dribble freely in the square - twisting, turning and changing speed.

- At the instruction of the coach, they then continue dribbling their footballs whilst performing any of the low-level plyometric drills.

- This could include hopping on the left foot whilst dribbling with the right foot, dragging the ball back with the sole of the left foot whilst hopping backwards on the right foot, hopping sideways (medially) on the left foot whilst dribbling with the outside of the right foot and so on.

- It is vital that the foot working the ball does not touch the ground.

- This is a very tiring exercise, so players should change hopping legs at least every 20 seconds.

- In between, they should dribble the ball normally, in order to aid recovery.

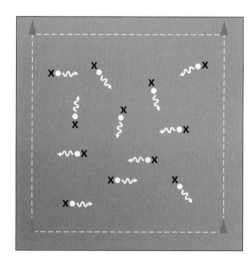

Exercise 55 >>>>>

Equipment: 4 cones, footballs and 6 bibs

Number of players: 12

Dimensions: 30m x 20m grid

The Game:

- A 30m by 20m grid is marked out with four cones.

- The players are divided into two groups of six, with one group in bibs. Each team has a ball.

- Players pass and move at random within their own group. However, when a rhythm has been established they quickly change to any of the low-level plyometric drills, as instructed by the coach.

- This could include passing with the right foot whilst hopping on the left foot, passing with the left foot whilst hopping on the right foot, passing with the right foot whilst hopping backwards on the left foot and so on.

- As this is a very tiring exercise, the coach should change the actions every 20 seconds.

- It is vital that the striking foot does not touch the ground whilst hopping.

- Random passing and moving can be used as the recovery period and should last for at least a minute between hopping actions.

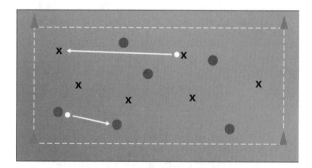

Progression

- The two teams of six now play 'keep ball' in the 30m by 20m grid.

- Each team plays to keep possession.

- At a signal from the coach, the players change to any low-level plyometric drill previously mentioned.

- This could include hopping backwards on the left foot, hopping forwards on the right foot and so on, whilst trying to maintain possession of the ball.

- Normal 'keep ball' should be played between actions in order to aid recovery.

Exercise 56 ⟫⟩⟩⟩⟩

Equipment: 16 cones, 12 footballs

Number of players: 12

Dimensions: 4 x 15m squares

The Game:

- Twelve players, each with a ball, dribble at pace within the grass square.

- They put in twists and turns, whilst maintaining control of their ball.

- Work for two minutes, and then take a minute's rest.

- The same action is repeated, but this time on shale.

- Work for two minutes, and then take a minute's rest.

- The action is repeated in the sandpit for two minutes, with a minute's rest.

- The final dribbling practice is carried out on the grassy slope.

- Work for two minutes. Give the players four minutes recovery, before repeating the whole practice.

Varying the environment helps to create total athletes. To improve balance, we need to play on uneven surfaces, alter our base stability and change the centre of gravity. We believe it is necessary to exaggerate the physical parameters, in order to improve them. We believe the above exercises, performed on different surfaces, go a small way towards creating better balanced and more rounded athletes.

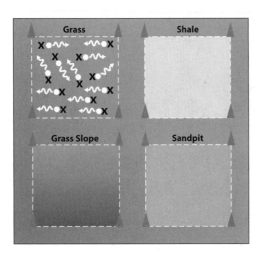

Variations

Instead of dribbling, the following activities could take place on the four surfaces:

- Juggling.

- Pass and move with three footballs.

- Volley out of the hand, with three footballs.

- Head out of the hand, with three footballs.

- Throw, control and catch, with three footballs.

- Dribbling a ball combined with strength exercises e.g. jumping backwards and forwards over the ball.

- Handball — two teams.

Rubber tubing, resistance, vision and balance

We have shown you how to use resistance as a means of developing balance, vision and decision-making, by combining low-level plyometric drills with realistic football actions. More resistance can be added to movement - to develop body control - by using rubber tubing. The tubing is secured around the player's shoulders and resistance created when held by another player. Old cycle inner tubes are a cheap yet effective way of creating resistance and most cycle repair shops are only too willing to donate their discarded tubes!

It is important that players know how to put the inner tube on. It is first placed along the back of the neck (making sure the valve does not dig in), across the shoulders and then underneath the arms.

The players should then practise using the rubber tubes before introducing a ball. It is essential that varying degrees of resistance are used, so that players experience various levels of body control. However, it is vital that not too much resistance is applied (the player can hardly move), or too little, since neither will have much effect on balance, vision or explosive power.

When a ball is introduced, teach players to receive it in four different positions. These are:

- On the ground
- Between the feet and hips
- Between the hips and the head
- Over the head

We want players to react to these four heights whilst using the inner tubes. Players will work in threes, with one working, one acting as feeder and one providing the resistance.

R◁X   ○F

The working player sprints six metres and receives a ground pass from the feeder, which he returns as quickly as possible, whilst being resisted by the tubing. This will challenge the player to keep body control, particularly if pulled slightly off-balance, as he is about to return the pass. The pull must be multi-directional (e.g. side to side and not just back) and the strength varied. The worker and his partner then jog back to the start and repeat the same explosive action five times. Players then change roles.

These actions are then repeated in the other three ball reception positions - between the feet and the hips, the hips and the head and above the head. In all positions, players have to work on balance in order to control their bodies and be able to return the ball as quickly as possible, with improvisation often being required.

Once players have practised receiving the ball from varying heights, with resistance, they are now placed in more functional situations.

Exercise 57 〉〉〉〉〉

The Game:

- ALL players start off wearing inner tubes, so that roles may be changed quickly.

- Five players work, five provide resistance and five act as feeders.

- Players move anywhere in the grid.

- The feeders throw balls at varying heights for the resisted players to return, with one or two touches.

- The partner holding the inner tube provides extra resistance when the worker is about to play the ball back.

- This helps develop explosive power and body control and often forces the player to improvise.

- The worker plays off as many feeders as possible in one minute.

- Players then change roles as quickly as possible in order to keep up the intensity of the exercise, with the feeder becoming the resister, the resister the worker and the worker the feeder.

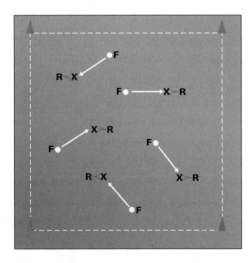

Exercise 58 〉〉〉〉〉

The Game:

- The players are divided into two groups of eight. One group wears a set of bibs and each group has a football.

- ALL players start off wearing inner tubes, so that roles may be changed quickly.

- Each team is divided into pairs, with one player working and the other resisting.

- The resisted players pass and move at random, within their own group.

- The partner holding the inner tube must provide varying degrees of resistance, so that the working player experiences different levels of body control, particularly when passing and controlling the ball.

- Players quickly change roles every minute.

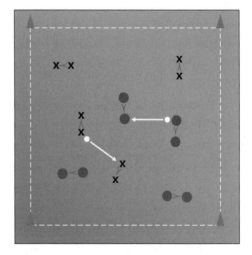

Progression One

- More experienced players may perform single-leg hops and pass the ball whilst being resisted.

- The partner resisting must continually try to get the worker off-balance, particularly as he is about to play the ball.

Progression Two

- The final progression is a game of 'keep ball' between the two groups.

- The aim is to try to throw the worker off-balance, rather than worry too much about who maintains possession.

- The worker and his partner change roles every minute.

We have placed the following three exercises in the aural, visual and balance section, although they are difficult to categorize. They are an innovative way of dealing with vision and communication, the latter being a problem which few coaches seem prepared to tackle.

Exercise 59 〉〉〉〉〉〉

Equipment: 14 eye patches, bibs and footballs

Number of players: 14

Dimensions: 60m x 40m grid

The Game:

- The players are divided into two teams, with one team in bibs.

- Team X wear eye patches on their left eyes and Team O wear eye patches on their right eyes.

- Play 'keep ball' for five minutes.

- At the end of five minutes, Team X wear the eye patches on their right eyes and Team O on their left eyes.

- Teams continue to play 'keep ball' for another five minutes.

- Finally, both teams remove the eye patches and continue the game for another 10 minutes.

- From our experience, once the patches are removed, players can more easily pick up the ball in their field of vision.

- We therefore feel that this is an innovative way to improve a player's vision and awareness.

Exercise 60 〉〉〉〉〉〉

Equipment: 14 ear plugs, set of bibs, 2 goals,

and footballs   Number of players: 14

Dimensions: 60m x 40m grid

The Game:

- The players are divided into two teams, with one team in bibs.

- In a normal 7 v 7 game, where goals can only be scored by hitting the net off the ground, Team X CANNOT talk or call for the ball.

- They may only communicate through signals or eye contact.

- Team O MUST give an instruction on every pass i.e. "man on", "open out" etc.

- If an instruction is not given, then a free kick is awarded to Team X.

- Play for five minutes and then change roles.

Variation

- Both teams choose a 'captain'.

- The 'captains' are the only players who are allowed to talk.

- All the other players may only communicate through signals or eye contact.

- A free kick is awarded against any player who talks, other than the 'captain'.

- Change the 'captains' regularly.

Progression

- To improve vision and communication skills further, Team X now wear ear plugs.

- This will place greater importance on visual communication and make balance more difficult.

- Team O play as normal.

- Work for five minutes, then Team O wear the ear plugs and Team X play as normal.

- Allow the teams a two-minute break, then both teams wear ear plugs for five minutes.

- Finally, both teams remove their ear plugs and play normal football for 10 minutes.

- Ask the players how much this exercise improved communication skills, both aural and visual.

Exercise 61 〉〉〉〉〉〉

Equipment: 4 cones, set of bibs and 2 footballs

Number of players: 14

Dimensions: 30m x 20m grid

The Game:

- The players are divided into two groups, with one group in bibs. Each group has a ball.

- Players pass and move at random within their own group.

- When a rhythm has been established, change the requirements. The player with the ball is only allowed to pass if he gets a call from a teammate AND eye contact is made.

- The call from the **receiving** player will either be 'one', 'two' or 'three'.

- If he calls 'one', it means that he wants the ball, if he calls 'two' it means that he doesn't want the ball and immediately checks out of the space and if he calls 'three' it means he wants to play a one-two with the passer.

- This is a simple way of making players communicate. Too many times young players say nothing or simply shout 'yes', often when hiding behind other players. This merely confuses the situation as no eye contact is made with the passer.

Progression

- For more experienced players add numbers 'four' and 'five'.

- 'Four' will require the player with the ball to pass to the receiver's right foot and 'five' to the receiver's left foot.

Vision and Colour

Vision is the most valuable and selective of the senses and attempting to observe the fast movements that occur in football places great demand on human vision. Football frequently takes place under different light conditions and because it is a dynamic sport, the constantly changing situations make it harder to discriminate objects and players, which can result in inaccurate information for the brain to process and lead to poor decision-making. The implication of this is that we need to use every method available to us in order to help players understand and see the game. One such method is the use of colour, but research suggests that we vastly under-utilise it as a way of learning the game and maintaining visual attention.

The U.S. military research and design budget is comparable to the entire UK defence budget. The U.S. military is extremely keen to identify factors that act as visual signatures, in order that their troops are able to remain invisible to the enemy. This has meant the complete redesign of the camouflage uniform and has formed the standard issue to all troops since Autumn 2005.

As the U.S. military has invested so much money and resources in researching vision, it would be remiss not to consider their findings. In sport and particularly football, we should be able to apply these principles to stress vision training, or reverse engineer them in order to aid vision.

With the latter in mind the three main principles of vision, according to the U.S. military, are colour, shape and texture, with colour being the most important. Bright colours and shiny materials or reflective strips could be used along with stripes, fixed lines or clearly defined geometric shapes on the shirts. Although the right colours, textures or shapes could aid vision, it is unlikely that professional clubs would adopt the ideas since the shirts would not be fashionable and so of little commercial value to the team. It is a pity that innovation is not put before profit occasionally.

We believe that the following exercises, which use colour as a means of improving tactical knowledge and peripheral and focal vision, will focus players' attention on the relevant visual cues and, by doing so, develop their visual acuity. Some of the exercises combine colour with balance and shape, so could be used in other sections of the book.

Equipment: 4 cones, 16 bibs (4 different sets)

Number of players: 16

Dimensions: 30m x 20m grid

The Game:

- The players are divided into groups of four, with each group wearing different coloured bibs.

- Each group is designated a colour to chase i.e. red chases blue, blue chases green, green chases yellow and yellow chases red.

- The players work for one minute and keep a running total of the number of players they touch.

- Each group then adds up its total, to find the winner.

- This is a great game for vision, as players have to be aware of the colour they are chasing, the colour chasing them and all the other players moving in the area.

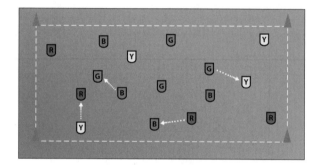

Variation

- Instead of wearing the bibs, players place them in the back of their shorts, so that part of them remains visible.

- As before, each group has a colour to chase and a colour chasing them and with the bib in the back of their shorts, a lot more twisting and turning occurs. Which colour collects the most bibs in one minute?

Exercise 63 ⟫⟩⟩⟩

Equipment: 4 cones, 2 sets of bibs

Number of players: 16

Dimensions: 30m x 20m grid

The Game:

- The players are divided into two groups of eight, with each group in different coloured bibs.

- The players place the bibs in the back of their shorts, so that part of it remains visible.

- The two groups compete against each other to take each other's bibs.

- The group that captures the most number of bibs is the winner.

Variation

- Fourteen players place the bibs in the back of their shorts, so that they are visible.

- The two players left act as the chasing pair.

- Any player who loses his bib automatically becomes a chaser.

- The number of chasers therefore rises constantly.

- The last two players to lose their bibs are the winners and become the chasers in the next game.

Exercise 64 ⟫⟩⟩⟩

Equipment: 16 hoops (4 x red, blue, green, yellow)

16 bibs (4 x red, blue, green, yellow)   Players: 16

Dimensions: penalty area

The Game:

- Sixteen players are divided into four groups, each group wearing different coloured bibs.

- Sixteen hoops are randomly scattered around the penalty area.

- The players have to put one foot in as many hoops as possible in 30 seconds.

- The players start off with one foot in their own colour but then must follow the sequence, red to blue, blue to green, green to yellow and yellow back to red.

- The coach should keep changing the colour sequence.

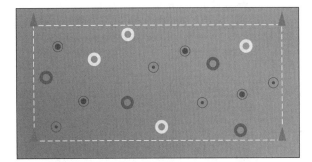

Variations

(Players work the 'Game' sequence as just mentioned but change the actions)

- Players put three small steps in each hoop.

- Players quick feet around each hoop.

- Players put one foot in each hoop and perform a header.

- Players sit down in each hoop.

- Players jump over each hoop and then step back into it.

- Players sprint to the first hoop, run backwards to the second, run sideways to the third and carioca to the fourth.

The possibilities are endless and are only limited by the imagination of the coach.

Exercise 65 ⟩⟩⟩⟩⟩

Equipment: 4 cones, 4 different coloured bibs and a football   Number of players: 5

Dimensions: 10m x 10m grid

The Game:

- A 10-metre square is marked out with four cones.

- Four players, wearing different coloured bibs, stand on each side of the square.

- The working player, in this case X, starts in the middle with the ball.

- X passes to blue, who returns the ball first time.

- As blue passes it back, he calls out another colour, (in this case red).

- X has to adjust his feet quickly and pass to red.

- Red returns the ball first time to X and as he does so, calls out another colour and the process continues.

- X works for one minute and then changes with one of the outside players.

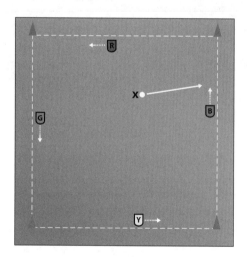

Progression

- To make the practice harder, the outside players jog slowly round the square.

- They must keep an equal distance apart and the coach should change the direction frequently.

Exercise 66 ⟩⟩⟩⟩⟩

Equipment: 4 cones, 4 red bibs, 4 blue bibs and footballs   Number of players: 8

Dimensions: 15m x 15m grid

The Game:

- A 15-metre square is marked out with four cones.

- Four players, two wearing red bibs and two wearing blue bibs, stand on opposite sides of the square.

- Two more pairs of players, each pair with a ball, start off in the middle.

- They pass to their partner and to either of their outside players, who must return the ball one touch.

- Once a pattern has been established, make the game harder by asking the outer players to jog slowly around the outside of the square.

- They should keep an equal distance apart and the coach should change the direction frequently.

- Work for two minutes and then change the roles.

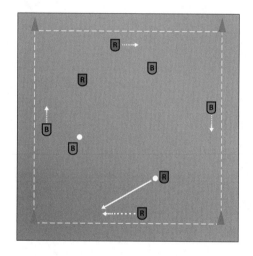

Progression One

- Play 2 v 2 in the middle, with both teams using their outside players for support.

- The outside players cannot be tackled, but are limited to two touches.

Progression Two

- In the second progression, the teams play 2 v 2 in the middle, whilst the outside players jog slowly around the square.

- The outside players cannot be tackled and are limited to two touches.

- Passes to the outside should either be to feet or in front of the receiver.

- Work for two minutes and then change roles.

Progression Three

- In the final progression, play two 1 v 1 games with both pairs using their outside players for support.

- As above, the outside players jog slowly round the square.

- This game is more strenuous and roles should be changed every minute.

Exercise 67 >>>>>>

Equipment: 4 different coloured cones,

2 sticks or chalk and 4 different coloured cards

The Game:

- A cross shape is marked out with two sticks or chalk.

- Each section is numbered 1, 2, 3 or 4.

- The four cones are placed five metres from the cross, as in the diagram.

- The player starts on marker 1 and performs the following two-footed jumps as quickly as possible.

  - 1 to 2
  - 1 to 4
  - 1 2 3
  - 1 2 3 4
  - 1 4 3 2

Repeat all the above on the left foot.

Repeat all the above on the right foot.

- Two-footed jumps, the player works for 20 seconds.

- One-footed jumps, the player works for 10 seconds.

At the end of each set of jumps, the coach calls out a colour and the player has to sprint to that coloured cone as quickly as possible.

The player rests for 30 seconds after the jumps and sprint.

Variation

- The coach calls out two colours, but the player has to sprint to the **first** colour that is called out. This will ensure extra concentration.

- Instead of calling out a colour, the coach holds up a coloured card. This will make players look up!

Exercise 68 >>>>>>

Equipment: 4 different coloured cones

2 markers and a football

Number of players: 2

The Game:

- Four different coloured cones are placed in a semi-circle, five metres apart.

- Two more markers, three metres apart, are placed in the middle of the semi-circle, as in the diagram.

- X starts at marker 1, runs forward to marker 2, backwards to marker 1 and so on, taking short, quick steps.

- At any time, the coach or partner calls out a colour and the player has to respond quickly, sprint around that coloured cone and back to the starting point, where the process starts again.

- After several goes, the players change roles.

Progression One

- To make it harder, the working player starts on marker 2, so that he has his back to the coloured cones.

- He runs forwards and backwards, taking short, quick steps, until the coach calls out a colour.

- He turns as quickly as possible (hopefully in the right direction), sprints around the correct cone and back to the starting point, where the process starts again.

Variation

- Vary the movement between markers 1 and 2. This could include lateral runs, lateral slides, carioca, single leg hops, ricochets (rapid two-foot jumps) etc, before the sprint around the coloured cone.

Progression Two

- The feeder stands at marker 1 and plays a ball backwards and forwards to his partner.

- After several passes the feeder stops the ball, calls out a colour and his partner sprints around the appropriate cone and back to the starting point.

- After several goes, change the roles.

Exercise 69 〉〉〉〉〉

Equipment: 4 cones, 3 footballs (one of a different colour) and a set of bibs   Number of players: 12

Dimensions: 30m x 30m grid

The Game:

- The players are divided into two groups, with one group in bibs.

- Each group has a ball. In addition, there is a third ball of another colour.

- X's pass their ball randomly amongst themselves whilst O's do the same thing.

- The coloured ball, however, is passed alternately between the groups. Thus, the ball will be passed from X to O, O to X and so on.

- Encourage players to call clearly, move about the grid with their heads up and to make eye contact before passing.

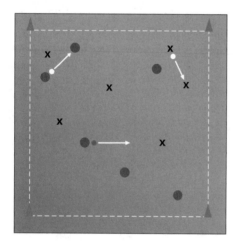

Variations

- Players have three touches with their own ball but only two with the coloured ball. This could be reduced to two touch and one touch, depending on the ability of the group.

- Players pass their own ball by feet, but the coloured ball is volleyed from the hand.

- Players pass their own ball by feet but the coloured ball is headed from the hand.

- Reverse the above so that the coloured ball is passed by feet whilst their own ball is headed or volleyed out of the hand.

Exercise 70 〉〉〉〉〉

Equipment: 4 cones, 4 different coloured balls

Number of players: 8 to 16

Dimensions: 30m x 20m grid

The Game:

- A 30m x 20m grid is marked out with four cones.

- The players start off randomly passing the four coloured balls amongst themselves.

- Once a rhythm has been established, the coach then asks for a different response from the players to each coloured ball. e.g. red ball - pass with the inside of the right foot, blue ball - pass with the inside of the left foot, green ball - pass with the outside of the right foot, white ball - pass with the outside of the left foot.

- To keep players focused, the coach should keep changing the response required for each coloured ball.

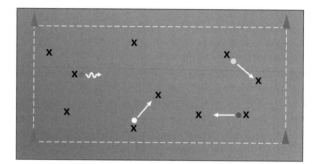

Variation One

- The players perform a different turn, according to the colour of the ball, before passing.

- Red ball - inside cut, blue ball - Cruyff turn, green ball - outside cut, white ball - drag back.

- For more experienced players it is possible to combine the turn and pass according to the colour of the ball e.g. red ball - inside cut and pass with the inside of the right foot, blue ball - Cruyff turn and pass with the inside of the left foot etc.

- The list is endless and the response required from the players to each coloured ball should be continually changed, so that they maintain concentration.

Variation Two

- The players perform a different take-over according to the colour of the ball.

- Red ball - normal take-over, blue ball - a drag back, yellow ball - outside cut into receiver's path, white ball - stop for receiver to run onto.

- It is essential that eye contact is made with the player about to perform the take-over.

- I would expect players to carry out movements such as feinting or sidestepping, prior to the take-over.

Exercise 71 ≫≫≫

Equipment: 4 cones, 5 balls (1 coloured)

and 4 sets of bibs   Number of players: 16

Dimensions: 40m x 30m grid

The Game:

- A 40m x 30m grid is set up with four cones.

- The players are divided into four groups, with each group wearing different coloured bibs.

- The players start off randomly passing four footballs amongst themselves.

- A coloured ball is then added, which has to be passed in sequence e.g. red bib to yellow bib, yellow to green, green to blue, blue back to red.

- The coach should keep changing the sequence, in order to keep the players focused.

Progression

- For more advanced players, a second coloured ball is introduced, which also has to be passed in sequence but different from the other coloured ball.

- The white balls are still passed randomly amongst the group.

- Once again, the coach should keep changing the sequence.

- If players struggle with this exercise, take out a white ball.

Exercise 72 ≫≫≫

Equipment: 4 cones and 4 coloured footballs

Number of players: minimum 12

Dimensions: 30m x 30m square

The Game:

- Players dribble four coloured balls, as fast as possible, before passing to a colleague.

- Once a rhythm has been established, add an additional activity to the dribble before passing.

- Red ball - player jumps to head a ball before passing, blue ball - player sits down and gets up before passing, green ball - player puts chest on the ground before passing, white ball - player jumps and turns 180 degrees before passing.

- Once a player has performed the agility, he must pass the ball within two touches.

- By having to concentrate on an additional activity, the basic task of passing and dribbling becomes much more difficult.

- It is essential that players keep control of the ball whilst performing the agility.

- To keep a high tempo, the dribble, agility and pass should take no longer than six seconds.

- The coach should keep changing the agility response required to each coloured ball, in order to keep the players focused.

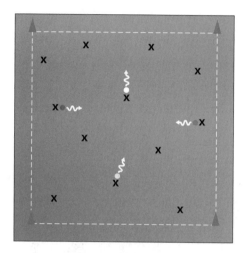

Variation

- Players run with the balls in their hands and throw them for the receivers to control and catch.

- However, before controlling the ball, the receiving player has to perform an agility.

- Red ball - sit down and get up, blue ball - back on the ground and get up, green ball - chest on the ground and get up, white ball - chest on the ground, back on the ground and get up.

- The ball should be thrown as the receiver is getting up from the ground, so that he has to control it off-balance.

- To make the practice harder, the receiver must jump in the air as he controls the ball.

Equipment: 16 cones of 4 different colours and 3 footballs   Number of players: 12

Dimensions: 25m x 15m grid

The Game:

- Twelve players randomly pass three footballs.

- After each pass they sprint to an outside cone and back into the game.

- However, a different action is required at each coloured cone.

- Red cone - quick feet around, blue cone - jump over and turn 180 degrees, yellow cone - spin behind, white cone - volley over the top.

- The coach should change the required response regularly, in order to keep the players focused.

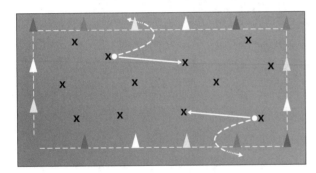

Progression

- Play 10 v 2, with the attacking players restricted to two touches.

- In all other respects, the practice is the same as outlined above.

- However, players must be aware of their position as they re-enter the game, in order to support the player on the ball.

Equipment: 4 different coloured footballs, 16 cones of 4 different colours   Number of players: 12 to 16

Dimensions: 25m x 15m grid

The Game:

- Twelve players randomly pass four different coloured footballs.

- After passing, they immediately sprint around a cone, which matches the colour of the ball passed i.e. pass a red ball, sprint round a red cone; pass a white ball, sprint round a white cone and so on.

- It is essential that the footballs and cones are matched for colour.

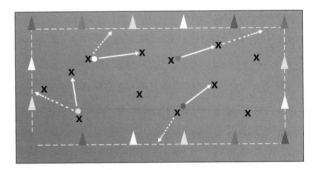

Progression

- When a pattern has been established, the coach asks for a different action from the players at each coloured cone e.g. pass the red ball and quick feet around the red cone; pass the blue ball and volley over the top of a blue cone; pass the white ball and jockey back three steps at a white cone; pass the green ball and jump over the top of a green cone.

- To keep the players focused, the coach should keep changing the actions required at the cones.

- To make the practice physically harder, the players sprint round two outside cones, but not on the same side.

Exercise 75 ⟩⟩⟩⟩⟩

Equipment: 24 cones (x 6 red, white, yellow, blue) and 16 footballs   Number of players: 16

Dimensions: 30m x 25m grid

The Game:

- Twelve small goals are set up with cones (three goals of each of the four colours above) and are placed around the field at different angles.

- The players have to sprint through as many goals as possible in 30 seconds.

- When a rhythm has been established, the players then follow a movement sequence suggested by the coach e.g. sprint to the first goal, run backwards to the second goal, shuffle sideways to the third goal, hop on the left foot to the fourth goal and hop on the right foot to the fifth goal.

- A movement sequence is then combined with a colour sequence e.g. sprint to a yellow goal, carioca to a white goal, run backwards to a blue goal and hop to a red goal.

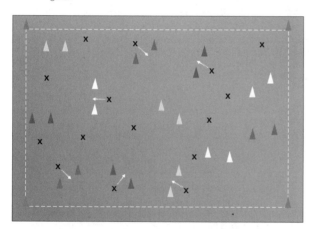

Progression One

- Each player has a ball and dribbles through the goals in any direction.

- They must keep the ball close to them, using the insides, outsides and soles of their feet.

- They should change pace and explode as they dribble through the goals.

- As they do so, they should call out "attacking space".

- On a signal from the coach, they should leave their football and continue sprinting through the goals and in and out of the footballs.

- On another signal, they collect the nearest football and continue dribbling at pace through the goals.

Progression Two

- The players follow a colour sequence called out by the coach e.g. red goal to blue goal, blue to white, white to yellow and yellow back to red.

- This will require players to look around and make decisions as, if one player is occupying a goal, the other players must look for another open goal.

- To make the task harder, insist that players perform a trick before exploding through the goal.

Exercise 76 ⟩⟩⟩⟩⟩

Equipment: 4 cones, 4 poles, 4 hurdles, 4 hoops and 3 different coloured footballs

Players: 12 to 16 Dimensions: 20m² inside 30m²

The Game:

- A 20m square is marked out with four cones.

- An outer 30m square is marked out with four hurdles, four poles and four hoops (see diagram). Footballs, ladders, slalom poles etc could also be used.

- Players randomly pass the three coloured footballs in the 20m grid.

- After passing the ball, the player must perform a task on the equipment, before rejoining the inner square.

- For example, if he passes a red ball, he must sprint and touch any pole.

- If he passes a white ball, he must jump over a hurdle.

- If he passes a green ball, he must quick feet around a hoop.

- Work for three minutes and then give the players an active rest, as this exercise is very demanding.

- To keep players focused, the coach should keep changing the actions required according to the colour of the football.

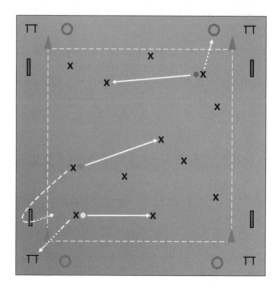

Exercise 77 》》》》

Equipment: 12 cones, 3 footballs + 1 of a different colour   Number of players: 15

Dimensions: 3 x 12m squares

The Game:

- Three x 12-metre squares are marked out as in the diagram and five players are placed in each square.

- Each group has a ball, which is randomly passed between them.

- A fourth ball of a different colour is passed from square to square and in any order.

- Players have to watch their ball, as well as the course of the coloured ball, particularly when they are passing.

- It is important that the two balls do not hit nor end up at the same player.

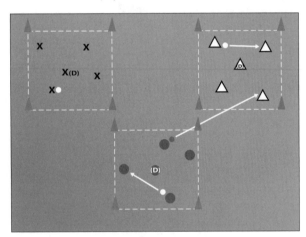

Progression

- One player from each group becomes a defender.

- A 4 v 1 situation is created and the attackers attempt to keep possession of their ball.

- The pressure on the attackers is intensified as the coloured ball still has to be passed amongst the three groups.

- If the players find this difficult, make the defender passive to start with.

- Work for two minutes, then change the defender.

Exercise 78 》》》》

Equipment: 4 cones, 8 hoops (2 x 4 colours), a football and a set of bibs   Number of players: 12

Dimensions: 60m x 40m grid

The Game:

- One hoop of each colour is placed at either end of the pitch.

- The players are divided into two equal teams, with one team in bibs.

- Each team attacks and defends a set of hoops.

- The aim is to stop the ball inside a hoop.

- Each hoop has a different value.

- Yellow - 4 points, red - 3 points, green - 2 points, blue - 1 point.

- To keep the players focused, the coach should regularly change the value of each coloured hoop.

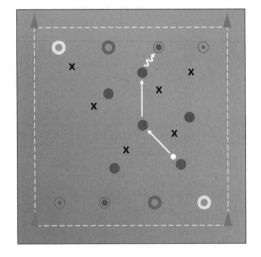

Variation

- Instead of putting the hoops in a line, place them randomly in each half.

Exercise 79 »»»

Equipment: 4 cones, 4 footballs, 4 sets of bibs

Number of players: 16

Dimensions: 30m x 30m square

The Game:

- The players are divided into four equal teams, each wearing different coloured bibs.

- Each team has its own ball.

- The teams randomly pass their ball from one teammate to another, making sure that all the spaces in the square are filled.

- When a rhythm has been established, players may also pass to a player of another colour, who must return the ball first time to the player who gave him the ball.

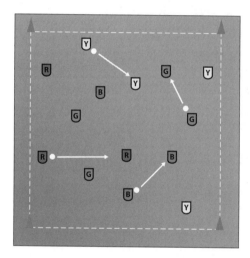

Progression One

- Players pass to another colour. The receiver has to return the ball to a player of the same colour that gave him the ball, but NOT to the original passer.

Progression Two

- At a signal from the coach, the teams form groups in the four corners of the square and continue passing and dribbling around the cones.

- At a signal from the coach, the players form four groups of different colours in each corner and continue passing and dribbling around the cones.

Exercise 80 »»»

Equipment: 4 cones, 4 footballs and 4 sets of bibs

Number of players: 16

Dimensions: 30m x 30m square

The Game:

- The players are split into four groups, with each group having a ball and wearing different coloured bibs.

- Players randomly pass the balls to any colour, but call out the colour they have passed to.

- When a rhythm has been established, the receiver also calls out the colour of the person who passed to him. These two activities should encourage players to play with their heads up.

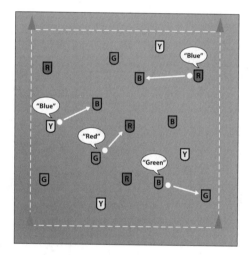

Progression

- Players call out the colour they are going to pass to, BEFORE they receive the ball.

- This is a difficult exercise, so should start with all players stationary.

- When the coach feels the players are comfortable, he should allow them to move slowly in the square.

- If necessary, take out two footballs at the start.

Variation

- Instead of calling out the colour, players call out the name of the person they are going to pass to, before receiving the ball.

- This is a difficult exercise and should be developed slowly.

Equipment: 4 cones 4 sets of bibs and 3 footballs

Number of players: 12

Dimensions: 30m x 20m grid

Equipment: 4 cones, 4 footballs and 4 sets of bibs

Number of players: 16

Dimensions: 30m x 30m grid

The Game:

- The players are divided into four equal groups, each wearing different coloured bibs.

- The players jog anywhere in the grid.

- Two players are designated 'starters' (Y1 and R1). They sprint and then touch any player in the area.

- As they touch the players, they call out a colour.

- The two touched players then become the chasers and must sprint and touch a player of the colour called out.

- This sequence then continues.

The Game:

- Players are split into four groups, with each group having a ball and wearing different coloured bibs.

- Players pass in sequence as stipulated by the coach i.e. red to yellow, yellow to blue, blue to green and green to red.

- To make players think, the coach should keep changing the sequence.

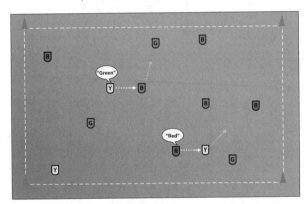

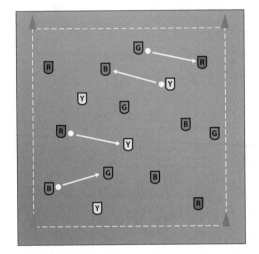

Progression One

- A player must not call out the colour of the player he touches e.g. if the player he touches is wearing a blue bib, he cannot call out 'blue'.

Progression Two

- When the chasing player calls out a colour, the touched player can touch any colour OTHER THAN the one called out.

Progression Three

- The touching player calls out a colour and short or long.

- If he calls out 'blue short', the touched player has to sprint to the nearest blue player.

- If he calls out 'blue long', the touched player has to sprint to the blue who is furthest from him.

- This is an excellent practice for scanning.

Progression Four

- Three footballs are now introduced.

- As before, the player passing the ball calls out a colour to the receiver.

- The receiver passes the ball to a player of that colour and, in turn, calls a colour for that player to pass to.

- This exercise is much more difficult than it appears, so players could start off passing by hand.

Progression One

- Players pass in sequence, but only have two touches and MUST use both feet.

- Quick support is essential for the player on the ball.

Progression Two

- Players pass in sequence, but two-touch play for two colours and one-touch play for the other two colours.

- To make this easier, players call out "one-touch" or "two-touch", as they pass to the next colour.

- This is a difficult game so start off with two footballs.

Exercise 83 ⟫⟫⟩⟩

Equipment: 4 cones, x 3 red, blue and green bibs and 2 footballs   Number of players: 12

Dimensions: 30m x 20m grid

The Game:

- The players are divided into three equal groups, each wearing different coloured bibs.

- Two of the colours (in this case red and green) have a ball each and pass to their own colour.

- In addition, both colours can pass to a blue and he has to return the ball first time.

- Work for three minutes and then change roles.

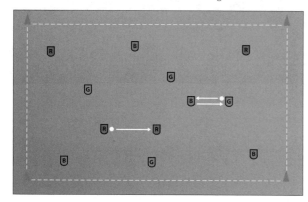

Variation

- Blue has to return the ball to the same colour that passed him the ball, but not to the same player.

Progression

- Two of the colours team up and attempt to keep possession of both footballs.

- If the defenders win a ball, they immediately return it to the attackers.

- Each defender keeps a record of how many times he wins a ball.

- After three minutes, change the defending team.

- Which defending team gains the most wins?

- This is an excellent game for improving peripheral vision, since attackers and defenders have to be aware of both footballs.

Exercise 84 ⟫⟫⟩⟩

Equipment: 1 football and 3 sets of bibs

Number of players: 9

Dimensions: 40m x 30m grid

The Game:

- The players are divided into three equal groups, with each group wearing different coloured bibs.

- There is one football per nine players.

- The players are spread randomly around the grid and remain stationary.

- The player with the ball passes to any colour and sprints after his pass, at maximum speed.

- When a rhythm has been established, stipulate that players may pass to any colour other than their own.

- Allow two touches to start with, but quickly get down to one-touch passing if the players are capable. This makes it a much more difficult exercise, both technically and visually.

- As players are working at maximum speed, work for one minute and rest for 30 seconds. Repeat a minimum of eight times.

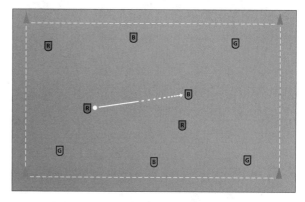

Progression

- Players pass to one colour, but sprint to any other colour in the grid e.g. red passes to green but sprints to a blue player.

- Since this is a very demanding exercise, allow two touches to start with and only progress to one touch if the players are capable.

Exercise 85 >>>>>>

Equipment: 4 cones, 1 football and 3 sets of bibs
Number of players: 12 to 18
Dimensions: 40m x 40m grid

The Game:

- The players are divided into three groups, with each group in different coloured bibs.

- Red and green work together to keep the ball away from yellow.

- If yellow win the ball, the team that gave the ball away become the defenders.

- Can the team working together make 10 consecutive passes?

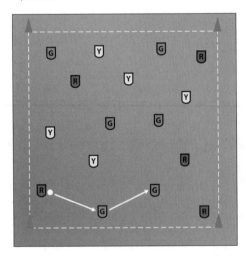

Variations

- Change the defending team every two minutes; the colour that regained possession most becomes the winner.

- Two-touch play for the attackers, but they must use both feet.

- The attacking teams must always pass to the opposite colour. Therefore, red always passes to green and green always passes to red. The number of passes are now halved, so players must work harder to support the player on the ball.

Exercise 86 >>>>>>

Equipment: 4 cones, 3 sets of bibs (red, green and blue) and 3 footballs   Number of players: 12
Dimensions: 30m x 20m grid

The Game:

- Players are divided into three teams, each having a ball and in different coloured bibs.

- Players start off juggling the ball on the move and passing to their own colour.

- Teammates must keep jogging when they don't have the ball, so that the juggler has to move in traffic.

- The juggler must also move his eyes away from the ball, in order to select the correct pass.

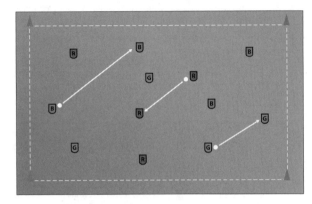

Progression One

- Players juggle the ball in traffic and pass in a fixed colour sequence e.g. green to blue, blue to red, red to green.

- The coach should keep changing the sequence.

Progression Two

- Players juggle the ball four or five times, stop it, then dribble at pace before passing.

- The receiver has to flick the ball up and then repeat the exercise.

- Once again the players should pass in a fixed colour sequence e.g. green to blue, blue to red and red back to green.

Progression Three

- For more advanced players, two colours are combined and they play keep ball against the other colour, thus creating an 8 v 4 situation.

- The attackers must juggle, pass and control the ball without using their hands.

- This is a very difficult exercise, so make the defenders passive. They may harass the player with the ball but not touch it.

- The aim for the attackers is to make sure the ball does not touch the ground.

- Work for three minutes, then change the defending team.

- When a rhythm has been established, allow the defenders to intercept the ball, but not touch it when the attacker is juggling or receiving it.

Exercise 87 ⟫⟫⟫

Equipment: 4 cones, 3 sets of bibs and footballs

Number of players: 11

Dimensions: 30m x 20m grid

The Game:

- The players are divided into two teams of four and one team of three.

- Each team wears different coloured bibs.

- Two teams combine and attempt to keep the ball away from the third team as long as possible.

- If the defenders win the ball, they must first dribble it out of the grid, before changing roles.

- As the teams are of different sizes, the situation is constantly changing.

- When the team of three are defending, it's an 8 v 3 situation, otherwise it is 7 v 4.

- To make players think and be visually aware, allow them to play freely when it's 7 v 4, but only two-touch when it's 8 v 3.

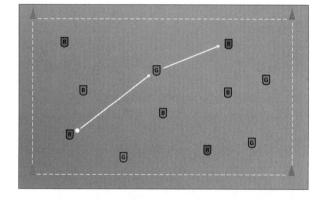

Exercise 88 ⟫⟫⟫

Equipment: 4 cones, 4 sets of bibs and 2 footballs

Number of players: 16

Dimensions: 40m x 40m square

The Game:

- The players are divided into four groups, with each group in different coloured bibs.

- The teams start by playing handball, with reds versus blues and greens versus yellows.

- Once a rhythm has been established, change to passing by feet.

- To make the players think, the coach should keep changing the pairings i.e. reds versus yellows and greens versus blues.

- It is useful if there is a coach to look after each game.

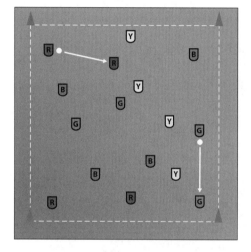

Progression

- Some direction is then put on the practice, with reds versus blues playing vertically and greens versus yellows playing horizontally.

- To score, players have to dribble over the end line they are attacking and place a foot on top of the ball.

- Once again, the coach should keep changing the pairings.

Exercise 89 ⟩⟩⟩⟩⟩

Equipment: 4 cones, 4 goals, 4 sets of bibs and 2 footballs   Number of players: 16

Dimensions: 40m x 40m square

The Game:

- Four small goals are placed centrally on the four sides of the grid, as in the diagram.

- The players are divided into four groups, each wearing different coloured bibs.

- Reds play yellows vertically and blues play greens horizontally, in two separate games.

- The coach should stipulate different ways of scoring e.g. one-touch finish, left foot only, header, hit the net off the ground, volley etc.

- To make players think, the coach keeps changing the pairings i.e. reds vs greens, blues vs yellows.

- It is useful if there is a coach for each game.

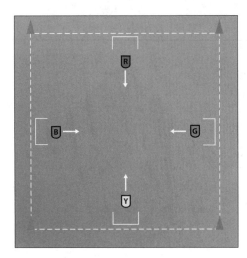

Progression One

- The four goals are now placed in each corner, so teams play diagonally.

- As before, two completely separate games are going on, on the same pitch.

- This particular game is excellent for vision, as players have to position themselves sideways on, in order to be aware of both goals.

Progression Two

- The colours are then joined, with reds playing with yellows and blues playing with greens.

- Each team now has two goals to attack and defend.

- Once again, this game is excellent for vision, as the player on the ball is encouraged to look around more, as there are two goals to attack. Teams should switch play if one route is blocked.

Exercise 90 ⟩⟩⟩⟩⟩

Equipment: 4 cones, 2 goals, 4 sets of bibs and 2 footballs   Number of players: 16 + 2 keepers

Dimensions: 50m x 35m grid

The Game:

- The players are divided into four groups, each wearing different coloured bibs.

- There is a goalkeeper in each goal.

- Two games are going on at the same time, on the same pitch, using the same goals.

- Reds versus blues and greens versus yellows, with reds and greens attacking the same goal and blues and yellows attacking the same goal.

- This is a very difficult game for the goalkeepers, as they always have to be aware of both footballs.

- Play for six minutes and then change the pairings i.e. reds versus yellow and greens versus blues.

- Award three points for a win and one for draw. When everybody has played each other, work out a league table.

- It is useful if there is a coach to referee each game.

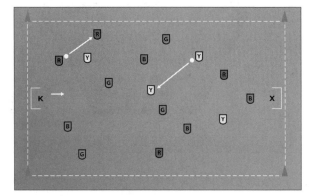

Progression

- Limit players to two touches. This makes the game very demanding as space is limited and players will have to be on the move constantly, in order to find support positions.

Exercise 91 >>>>>

Equipment: 4 cones, 2 goals, 4 sets of bibs and a football   **Number of players: 12**

Dimensions: 40m x 40m square

The Game:

- The players are divided into four groups, each wearing different coloured bibs.

- The colours are joined, with reds working with yellows and blues working with greens.

- The teams play 'keep ball' and score a point for completing eight consecutive passes.

- The teams are then made to pass in sequence i.e. red to yellow, yellow to red and blue to green, green to blue.

- This halves the number of passing options available and makes the game far more difficult.

- Work for five minutes and then change the pairings.

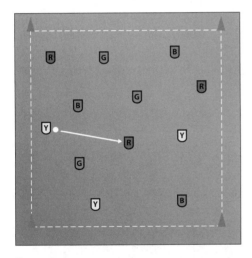

Progression

- The teams now attack a line or goal, but only ONE of the colours can score i.e. reds for one team and greens for the other.

- The coach should keep changing the pairings and which colour can score.

Exercise 92 >>>>>

Equipment: 8 cones, 4 sets of bibs and footballs

Number of players: 12 to 16

Dimensions: 60m x 40m grid

The Game:

- A 60m x 40m grid is marked out with a goal at each corner, as in the diagram.

- The players are divided into four groups, each wearing different coloured bibs.

- The colours are combined, with reds playing with yellows and blues playing with greens.

- The teams have two goals to attack and two goals to defend.

- Having two wide goals to attack should encourage players to switch play and change direction if one route is blocked.

- This in turn should make players get their heads up and look around more.

- The coach should keep changing the pairings.

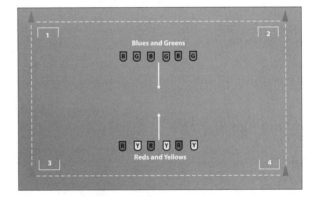

Progression One

- Stipulate different ways to score for each colour e.g. reds and blues can only score by dribbling through the goals whilst greens and yellows can only score on a one-touch finish.

Progression Two

- Each colour is restricted to which goal they can score in e.g. reds can only score in goal 1, yellows in goal 2, greens in goal 3 and blues in goal 4.

Progression Three

- Place a goalkeeper in goals 2 and 4. Teams score as normal where there is a goalkeeper, but can only score from headers in the unguarded goals.

Progression Four

- Teams attack two diagonal goals and defend two diagonal goals.

Exercise 93 ⟫⟫⟫

Equipment: 16 cones, 3 sets of bibs and footballs

Number of players: 9 to 12

Dimensions: 40m x 20m grid

The Game:

- A 40m x 20m grid is marked out with four cones.

- Six small goals are placed on opposite touch lines, as in the diagram and numbered 1, 2 or 3.

- The players are divided into three teams, each wearing different coloured bibs.

- Each team is given two goals to defend and four to attack. In this case, red defend goals 1, blue goals 2 and green goals 3.

- The aim is for the teams to play with each other and attempt to score in any goal other than the ones they are defending.

- They can pass to any player in their team or in any other and should be continually trying to create 6 v 3 situations.

- With four goals to attack, players should be looking to switch play continuously.

- Teams have to make sure that they don't lose possession near either of the goals they are defending.

- To speed the game up, play two-touch.

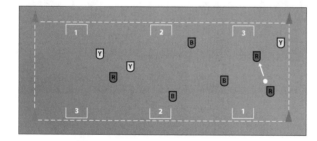

Exercise 94 ⟫⟫⟫

Equipment: 4 small goals, 4 cones, 4 sets of bibs and footballs   Number of players: 12 + 4 keepers

Dimensions: 40m x 40m square

The Game:

- A 40-metre square is marked out with four cones.

- Four small goals are placed in the middle of each touch line, as in the diagram.

- The players are divided into four teams, each wearing different coloured bibs.

- Each team is designated a goal to defend.

- The aim is for the teams to play with each other and attempt to score in any goal, except the one they are defending.

- They can pass to any player in their own team or in any other and should be continually looking to create 9 v 3 situations.

- If a team concedes a goal, they have to remove a player from the field and play with two players.

- If another goal is scored, the player is allowed back on the field and replaced by a player from the team that has just conceded a goal.

- Teams have to make sure that they don't lose possession near their own goal.

- With three goals to attack, players should be looking to switch play, changing direction if one goal is blocked.

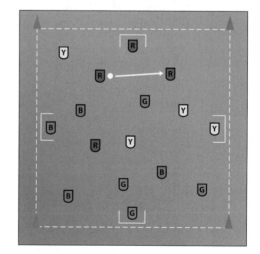

Scanning

In football, visual search is a vital part of the decision-making process. It involves looking for information, which will enable the player to decide what to do in any situation. Appropriate search strategies are vital for footballers, particularly when there is little time to make the decision and then carry out the action. Teaching players how to pre-scan, post-scan and scan whilst in possession is essential and, if taught properly, should bring about a marked improvement in their performance.

Players need to understand that planning in advance leads to time and space on the ball. The pre-scan process starts as soon as a player moves in support of a teammate. As the ball is passed to him, he must observe where it is coming from and how is it coming (on the ground, in the air, quickly, slowly etc). He must then look beyond the ball and select a response based on the present position and predicted movement of players around him. Simultaneously, he must decide where his first touch will be placed. As he receives the ball he should quickly glance at it and either pass it with one touch to the area chosen on the pre-scan or move it into space in order to gain time. Post-scanning now takes place, so that the player can check that the original decision was correct. If it was, then he should continue with the initial plan. If not, then he should modify the action and make an alternative pass or buy himself time by moving the ball into space, away from his current position and nearby opponents. If he chooses this option, then he must now scan whilst in possession in order to gain more time to make further decisions.

Once he has passed the ball, he must move quickly to provide support for others in possession, so that he is in a position to receive the ball again. He must avoid admiring the pass or standing still, as this effectively takes him out of the game. As the ball is travelling to a teammate, he should be moving again to support the next pass.

We believe the following games will help improve visual search strategies, as they will force players to scan prior to and after reception of the ball. It is essential that players understand that the information needed to solve game problems is all around them and NOT written on the ball.

Exercise 95 ⟫⟩⟩⟩⟩

Equipment: 4 cones, 2 footballs
Number of players: 12
Dimensions: 40m x 25m grid

The Game:

Pre-scanning

- Two footballs are passed randomly amongst the group.

- When a rhythm has been established, players call out the name of the player they have received from.

- Progress to calling out the colour of the shirt of the player they received from.

- The receiver calls out the name of the player closest to him, other than the passer.

- The receiver calls out the name of the player he is going to pass to before touching the ball.

- This is a difficult exercise and should start with the players stationary.

- All of the calls should be made prior to ball reception.

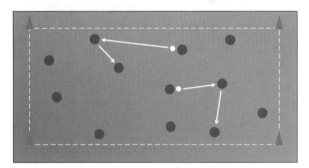

Post-scanning and scanning whilst in possession

- After selecting where the first touch should be played, the receiver dribbles the ball and calls out the name of the player furthest from him.

- The receiver calls out the name of a player behind him, either on his right or left, before passing.

Exercise 96 ⟫⟫⟫⟫

Equipment: 4 cones, 2 footballs and 12 (4 sets of 3 different colours) bibs   Number of players: 12

Dimensions: 40m x 30m grid

The Game:

Pre-scan

- The players are divided into four teams of three, each team wearing different coloured bibs.

- Two footballs are randomly passed about the group.

- Once a rhythm has been established, players call out the colour of the person they have received from.

- The receiver calls out the colour closest to him, apart from the passer.

- The receiver calls out the colour he is going to pass to **before** he receives the ball.

- This is a difficult exercise and should be started from a stationary position.

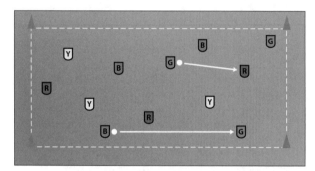

Post-scanning and scanning whilst in possession

- Whilst in possession, players call out the name of the player in their team who is furthest away.

- Call out the colour they have passed to.

- Call out the colour of the player closest to the person they have passed to.

- Pass in sequence e.g. red, to yellow, to blue, to green and back to red, but to the player in that colour furthest away.

Progression

- One team is now chosen as passive defenders, creating an 8 v 4 situation.

- The team of eight attempts to keep the ball, but players are not allowed to pass to the player nearest to them.

- The receiver calls out the name of the defender closest to him.

- The receiver calls out the colour he is going to pass to before he receives the ball.

- This is an advanced exercise and should only be used with experienced players.

Exercise 97 ⟫⟫⟫⟫

Equipment: 4 cones, 2 footballs (1 coloured) and 2 bibs   Number of players: 10

Dimensions: 25m x 20m grid

The Game:

- Eight attackers play against two defenders, who are passive.

- The attackers attempt to keep possession of both footballs.

- However, the defenders only defend against the white ball; they do not defend against the coloured ball.

- By continually scanning the field, the attackers should always be aware of the position of both footballs.

- Once a player has passed one ball, he should be looking to support the second one.

- Change the defenders every four minutes.

- Change the response required from both footballs i.e. defenders attack the coloured ball instead of the white one.

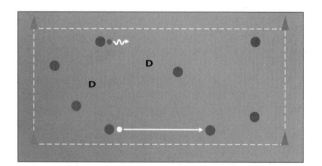

Progression

- Reduce the number of attackers from eight to six.

- Players will now be required to scan better and show quicker speed of thought.

- Insist on two touches only for the coloured ball.

- Finally, allow the defenders to become active, but only against the white ball.

- This practice should only be used with more experienced players.

Exercise 98 〉〉〉〉〉

Equipment: 4 cones, 4 bibs and footballs

Number of players: 12

Dimensions: 30m x 25m grid

The Game:

- Eight attackers v four defenders. Each defender wears a bib.

- The defenders each mark one attacker and **both** players stand still.

- The four unmarked attackers dribble the ball and pass **only** to unopposed players.

- The defenders should keep changing who they are marking every few seconds, in order to create new attacking situations for the attackers.

- Change the defenders every few minutes.

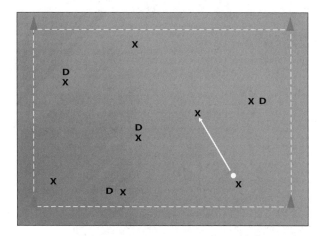

Progression

- The four marked attackers can now move, along with the defenders.

- To make it realistic, those being marked should change pace, check out, check in etc as they would in a game.

- The four unmarked attackers can still only pass to unopposed players.

- The defenders should change who they are marking every few seconds.

- This now becomes a difficult exercise and requires quick reactions, peripheral vision, awareness and the ability to scan the field prior to ball reception and whilst in possession.

Vision, Colour and the Head Up Hat

We know that over 90% of all the information that comes to the brain is visual, so we can help utilise the brain's visual systems' best qualities, with the use of colour and shape. We therefore need to help young players focus their attention on important cues, which, in turn, should lead to better and faster decision making.

With this in mind, we have developed the Head Up Hat, which is designed to make players of all standards play with their head up. The hat has a bright, fluorescent colour on one side, but can be turned inside out, where it is split into two contrasting colours. When using the surface of the hat with these contrasting colours, we stipulate that players pass to the dark or light side. This will greatly improve visual attention and provide youngsters with a better understanding of left and right - which many young players find difficult. The hats will improve decision-making, awareness and perception and help the individual become a better team player. In addition, peripheral vision will also be improved as the hats will encourage players to move their focus from the ball to the target, at the moment of contact or even before. This will train the players to have a better feel for the ball, as they are less likely to look down at it.

We have devised a programme of activities and invasion games to be used with this training aid, which will help the coach get the best out of this new, original idea. We are sure that, with a little imagination, coaches will be able to come up with their own ideas and practices.

Activities using the Head Up Hat

Key:

Fluorescent yellow | Fluorescent orange | Red/Black | Blue/Grey

Equipment: 16 Head Up Hats, 4 footballs, 4 cones

Number of players: 16

Dimensions: 25m x 25m square

The Game:

- The players are divided into two groups, each group having two footballs and wearing different coloured hats.

- Players start off passing by hand and to their own colour, but quickly change to passing by feet.

- Once a flow has been established, players may also pass to a player of another colour, who must return the ball first time to the player who gave him the ball.

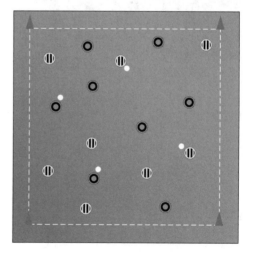

Progression

- Players pass in sequence i.e. orange hat to yellow hat, yellow hat to orange hat etc.

- After passing the ball the player should sprint out of the space, before looking for another ball.

Exercise 100 〉〉〉〉〉

Equipment: 16 Head Up Hats, 2 goals, 4 cones and footballs　　**Number of players: 16 max**

Dimensions: 40m x 35m grid

The Game:

- Play 8 v 8, with both teams wearing different coloured Head Up Hats.

- The teams play 'keep ball' and attempt to make six consecutive passes.

- However, they only score a point if the sixth pass is chipped to a team member and is caught. If the ball is dropped, the score does not count.

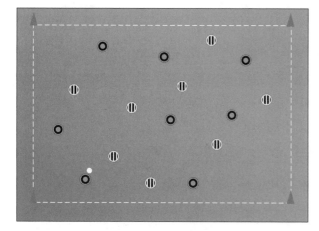

Progression

- Each team attacks and defends a six-a-side goal. There are no goalkeepers.

- The attacking team tries to progress the ball quickly and shoot in the opponents' goal. The ball must hit the net off the ground for the goal to count and it cannot bounce.

Exercise 101 〉〉〉〉〉

Equipment: 16 Head Up Hats, 4 cones and balls

Number of players: 16 max

Dimensions: 30m x 25m grid

The Game:

- The players are divided into four groups, each group having a football and wearing the four different coloured Head Up Hats.

- Players start off passing by hand and to their own coloured hats.

- Once a flow has been established, quickly change to passing by feet.

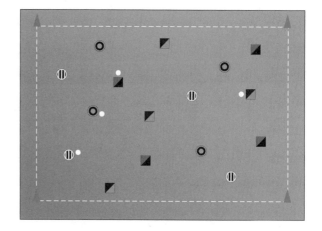

Progression

- Players can pass to any coloured hat, but must call out the colour of the hat they are passing to.

- At the same time, the receiver calls out the colour of the hat he has received from.

- For more advanced players, the player receiving the ball calls out the coloured hat he is going to pass to BEFORE he receives the ball. This is known as 'playing in the future'.

Exercise 102 〉〉〉〉〉

Equipment: 12 Head Up Hats, footballs and 4 cones

Number of players: minimum of 12

Dimensions: 30m x 25m grid

The Game:

- Players wear the Head Up Hats, with two colours showing (red/black and blue/grey).

- Teams start off passing by hand and to their own colours. Once a rhythm has been established, change to passing by feet.

- The players then pass in sequence, red/black to blue/grey, blue/grey to red/black.

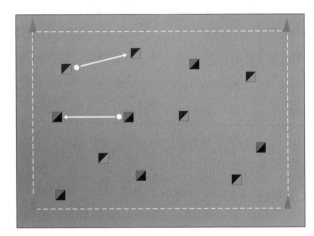

Progression

- The coach calls out dark or light and players have to pass to that side. If 'dark' is called out, then for the blue/grey hats that means passing to the right foot and for the red/black hats, to the left foot.

- The ball is passed in sequence i.e. dark side, light side, dark side. The passer must call out 'light' or 'dark' as the ball is played.

- Pass in order - blue to red to grey to black and back to blue. To make players think, the coach should keep changing the sequence.

Exercise 103 〉〉〉〉〉

Equipment: 12 Head Up Hats, footballs and 4 cones

Number of players: minimum of 12

Dimensions: 40m x 30m grid

The Game:

- The players are divided into four groups, with each group wearing a different Head Up Hat.

- The teams start by playing handball, with yellow versus red/black and orange versus blue/grey.

- Once a flow has been established, change to passing by feet.

- To make players think, the coach should keep changing the pairings.

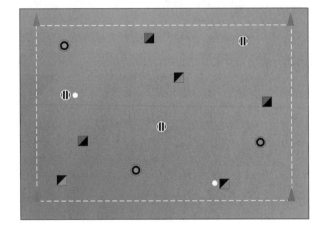

Progression

- Some direction is then put on the practice, with yellow versus red/black playing vertically and orange versus blue/grey playing horizontally. To score, players have to dribble over the end line they are attacking and place a foot on top of the ball. Once again, the coach should keep changing the pairings.

- The colours should then be joined, with yellow playing with red/black and orange playing with blue/grey. Start with 'keep ball' and progress to end ball.

For more advanced players, the ball must be passed in sequence - thus yellow will pass to red/black, red/black to yellow and orange to blue/grey, blue/grey to orange.

Vision and Shape

Small-sided games provide young players with a simple framework within which the coach can help them play the game. The smaller number of players and tighter playing area give them the chance to improve their ball skills, as they are constantly touching the ball. It also enables them to recognise the situations themselves and come up with their own solutions to problems. It is vital that players are able to think on their feet and make appropriate decisions based on the needs of the situation.

However, too often these small-sided games are played on pitches 60 metres long and 40 metres wide. In many ways, this is unrealistic to the game, since in an 11 a-side match, the distance between both full backs is often 60 metres or more whilst the distance between defenders and forwards is often no more than 40 metres. Therefore, why not play on a pitch which is 60 metres wide and 40 metres long? This is much more realistic to the game and allows for wing play, which is not possible on the normal shaped pitch.

We feel coaches should go even further and experiment with a wide variety of field shapes. For example, why not use circles, squares, triangles, diamonds, pentagons and hexagons? By moving away from a rigid pitch structure to a variety of shapes and sizes, the players will have to make continuous adjustments, as conditions will never be the same. This, in turn, will provide players with a good understanding of the field of play and help them to learn the inside and outside limits of the pitch. Once a player can find his bearings, he can now start positioning himself with regard to the ball, teammates and opponents.

We know, however, that from a tactical point of view, young players tend to group around the ball during these games. It is important that their tactical education develops from this, to a position where the player has an idea of time, space, shape and distance, with regards to his teammates, the opposition and the ball. One method of introducing basic tactics in a fun way is to divide the players into groups and then ask them to form certain geometric shapes. Explain that these shapes are ones that will always be found on the football pitch and could include the following:

Triangle

Square

Rectangle

Diamond

Diagonal

File

Line

Exercise 104 〉〉〉〉〉

Equipment: 4 cones, 3 sets of bibs and 3 footballs

Number of players: 12

Dimensions: 30m x 20m grid

The Game:

- A 30-metre by 20-metre grid is marked out with four cones.

- The players are divided into three teams of four, each team having a ball and in different coloured bibs.

- The teams carry out a series of passes using their hands. The ball must not touch the ground.

- It is important that visual contact is made between the person with the ball and the receiver.

- When a pattern has been established, the coach then instructs each team to organise itself into a precise formation such as a line, file, square, diagonal, rectangle, diamond or triangle.

- This will emphasise the need for group cooperation, as well as the ability of the player in possession of the ball, to organise his team.

- After a while, change to passing by feet.

- It is important that the coach recognises any mistakes in the shape or distance and quickly corrects them.

Variations

- Players sit or lie down in the shape instructed by the coach.

- Different ways of passing can be used i.e. bounce pass, volley from the hand, pass along the ground and flicked up, header from the hand etc.

- Players can pass in sequence e.g. red to blue, to green to red etc, but still get into the shape suggested by the coach, in their own team.

- Get one team to form a shape and the other team to defend that shape.

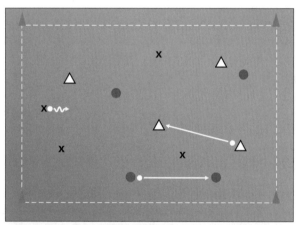

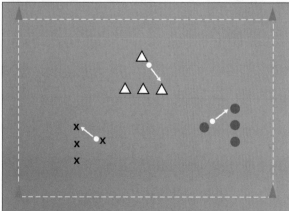

Vision and Shape

Exercise 105 >>>>>

The Game:

- Once players have practised the various shapes in a static position (as in the previous exercise), they then progress to maintaining shape whilst moving.

- The players are divided into groups of four and start in a diamond shape.

- They jog forward, keeping the starting distance and shape.

- This is not easy at first, so players must watch each other, talk and run at equal speed.

- In order to improve their visual perception, it is important that players experience every position in the diamond.

- Once players are able to control the distance and shape, they should then vary the speed.

- This will be controlled by player 2, who directs the group from the back, gives orders and adapts his position to those of his teammates.

- On the return journey, player 1 should take control and give the orders.

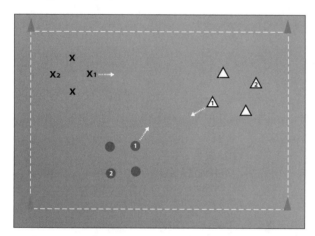

Progression

- The various shapes from the previous exercise should then be attempted, first of all moving slowly and then with a change of pace.

- Once this has been achieved, get the players to change to the shape that the coach calls out. Thus, they could change from a diamond to a rectangle and then to a diagonal, whilst still moving forwards.

Exercise 106 >>>>>

Equipment: 12 footballs
Number of players: 12
Dimensions: Half a pitch

The Game:

- The players are divided into groups of four, start in a diamond shape and have a ball each.

- They dribble their ball forwards, keeping the starting distance and shape.

- This is quite a difficult task, so players must watch each other, talk and dribble at equal speed.

- In order to improve their visual perception, it is important that players experience every position in the diamond.

- Once players are able to control the distance and shape, they should then vary the speed.

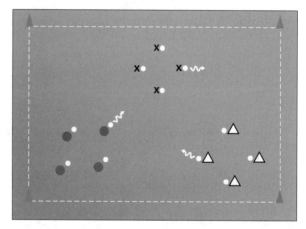

Progression One

- The various shapes from the previous exercise should then be attempted, first of all dribbling slowly and then with a change of pace.

- Once this has been achieved, get the players to change to the shape that the coach calls out. Thus, they could change from a diamond to a square and then to a file, whilst still moving forwards.

- To improve visual perception and communication whilst dribbling, allow more advanced players to change positions whenever they wish, whilst still maintaining the designated shape.

Progression Two

- In the final progression, only one football is used.

- The players move forwards in the shape designated by the coach.

- Whilst moving, they pass the ball amongst themselves and change position, but still keep the correct shape.

- This is a very difficult task, as it will involve the correct timing and weight of pass whilst on the move.

- Once a pattern has been established, the coach must ensure that the change of position is performed at speed.

- This exercise will test perception and communication as well as good ball control and accuracy of pass.

Exercise 107 »»»»»

Equipment: 4 cones, 4 sets of bibs and 4 footballs

Number of players: 12

Dimensions: 40m x 30m grid

The Game:

- The players are divided into four groups of three players, each group with a ball and in different coloured bibs.

- Players move within the grid and pass in triangles.

- They should vary the distance of the passing.

- Players can come short, then spin away to receive long passes or run away long and check back short for a ball to feet.

- The third player must always move early to create a support position and at the correct angle, so that the second player has the choice of laying the ball off first time.

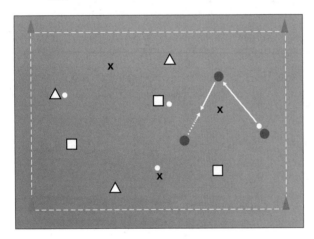

- The coach should keep emphasizing the triangular shape. Change the end player every two minutes.

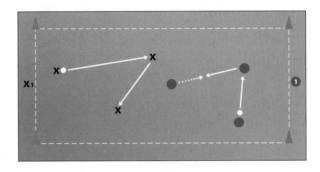

Progression One

- The player who passes to his own end player takes his place.

- When the ball is passed to the end player, anybody **other** than the passer takes his place.

Progression Two

- Move to 3 v 3, with both teams attacking a goal or target.

- If goalkeepers are available, use them. If not, place a large cone in the centre of each goal, which acts as the target.

Exercise 108 »»»»»

Equipment: 4 cones, 2 sets of bibs and 2 footballs

Number of players: 6 + 2

Dimensions: 40m x 20m grid

The Game:

- The players are divided into two groups of four, each with a ball and in different coloured bibs.

- One player from each team is placed behind an end line, as in the diagram and acts as a target player.

- X's work the ball up the pitch, pass to O1, then reverse their direction of play and attack the opposite end line, where they finish with a pass to X1.

- O's do the same in the opposite direction. Both teams pass through each other.

- All players should touch the ball at least once, before the ball is passed to an end player.

Vision and Shape

Exercise 109 ⟩⟩⟩⟩⟩

Equipment: 3 cones, 3 sets of bibs and footballs

Number of players: 9

Dimensions: 25m equal-sided triangle

The Game:

- The players are divided into three groups of three players, each group wearing different coloured bibs.

- Groups X and O play 3 v 3 inside the triangle and try to keep possession of the ball.

- The players from group A stand at the corners of the triangle and are used as support.

- Two teams switch roles every two minutes.

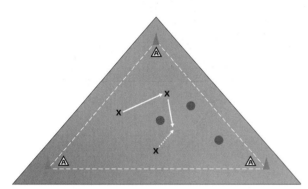

Variations

- All players are limited to two touches.

- X and O have unlimited touches, but A players are restricted to one touch.

- A must not pass back to the player that gave him the ball.

Exercise 110 ⟩⟩⟩⟩⟩

Equipment: 12 cones, 3 sets of bibs and footballs

Number of players: 9

Dimensions: 30m x 25m grid

The Game:

- The players are divided into three equal groups, each group wearing different coloured bibs.

- The diagram explains the position of the players.

- Team A can score in goals 3 and 4.

- Team O can score in goals 1 and 2.

- Team X scores a point each time a player controls the ball on the lines **between** goals 1-2 and 3-4.

- Work for five minutes, then change the goals that the teams are attacking.

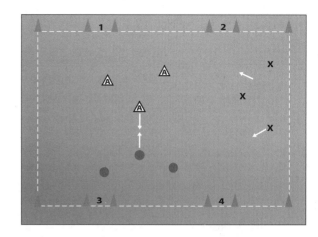

Exercise 111 ⟩⟩⟩⟩⟩

Equipment: 4 cones, a set of bibs and footballs

Number of players: 6

Dimensions: 40m x 30m grid

The Game:

- Four players, in a basic diamond shape, work up and down the pitch, passing to each other and to two target players (T1 and T2).

- The target players could be goalkeepers.

- This shape gives players all the passing possibilities found in the full game. i.e. forwards, backwards and sideways.

- Players in positions 2 and 3 need to understand that they must always be sideways on, facing into the field, with their back to the touch line.

- Once players are able to keep the diamond shape, the coach should encourage greater movement within the shape i.e. takeovers, overlaps, wall passes, set up plays, diagonal runs etc.

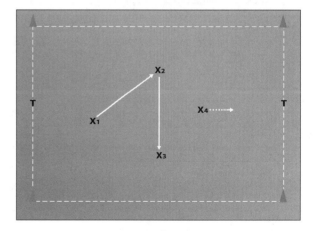

Progression

- When the coach is satisfied that the players understand the shape, introduce another team and have them play through each other, using them as non-competitive opponents.

Exercise 112 ⟩⟩⟩⟩⟩⟩

Equipment: 4 cones, 2 sets of bibs and footballs

Number of players: 8

Dimensions: 40m x 25m grid

The Game:

- The players are divided into two groups of four, with each group in different coloured bibs.

- This is now a competitive 4 v 4 game.

- To score, a player must dribble the ball over the goal line, under control.

- The attacking team should spread out as wide and long as possible, so they are difficult to mark.

- They should attempt to maintain a rough diamond shape, in order to ensure good angles and a wide range of passing possibilities.

- The defending team becomes a diamond within the opponents' attacking diamond, as in the diagram.

- As the attackers move, the defending team must move to compensate.

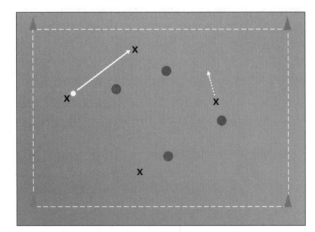

Progression

- Place a goal or target on the goal line.

- Both teams should still try to maintain a rough diamond shape, whether attacking or defending.

Exercise 113 ⟩⟩⟩⟩⟩⟩

Equipment: 4 cones, 3 sets of bibs and footballs

Number of players: 12

Dimensions: 25m x 4 grid

The Game:

- The players are divided into three groups of four, each group wearing different coloured bibs.

- Two teams (X and O) work inside the diamond shape and play 4 v 4.

- The team in possession attempts to keep the ball and complete eight consecutive passes.

- The third team (Y) are placed at the four points of the diamond and act as support for the team in possession. This creates an 8 v 4 situation.

- Y's are limited to two touches and cannot be tackled.

- Work for three minutes and then change roles.

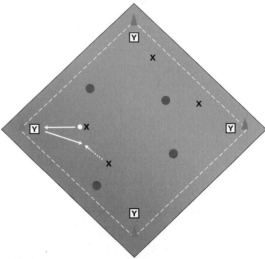

Variation

- The support players stand on the four sides of the diamond (as in diagram 2).

- They may move up and down their side of the diamond.

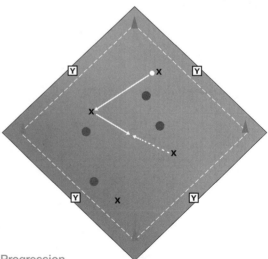

Progression

- When the team in possession completes six passes in a row, the losing team sprints to the outside of the diamond and the support team sprints in to take their place.

- The winning team continues passing whilst the changeover is taking place.

- It is therefore vital that the incoming team reacts very quickly, in order to maintain the intensity of the exercise.

Exercise 114 ⟫⟫⟫⟫⟫

Equipment: 6 cones, set of bibs, markers and footballs   **Number of players: 12**

Dimensions: 40m x 30m grid

The Game:

- The players are divided into two teams, with one team wearing bibs.

- A diamond shape is marked out inside the grid, as in the diagram.

- Two large cones are used as goals.

- A player from each side is allowed inside the diamond shape, whilst the rest of the players have to keep to their own areas.

- This pattern makes sure that teams play wide during mid-field play and scope is given to wing and full back play.

- By restricting players to the shape below, they get a better idea of marking, particularly when possession is lost.

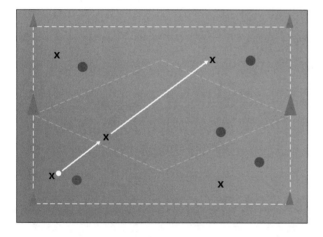

Exercise 115 ⟫⟫⟫⟫⟫

Equipment: 5 cones, 3 sets of bibs and footballs

Number of players: 15

Dimensions: 25m x 5

The Game:

- The players are divided into three groups of five, each group wearing different coloured bibs.

- Two teams (X and Y) work inside the pentagon and play 5 v 5.

- The attacking team aims to keep possession and complete eight consecutive passes.

- The third team (O) are placed at the five points of the pentagon and act as support players for the team in possession.

- They are limited to two touches and cannot be tackled.

- Work for four minutes and then change roles.

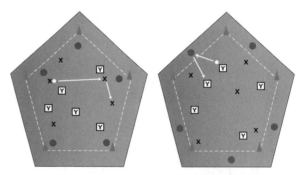

Variation

- The support players stand on the sides of the pentagon.

- They may move up and down on their side of the shape but only between the cones.

Progression

- When the team in possession completes six consecutive passes, the losing team sprints to the outside of the pentagon and the support team sprints in to take their place.

- The winning team keeps passing whilst the change-over takes place.

- It is therefore vital that the incoming team reacts very quickly, in order to maintain the intensity of the exercise.

Exercise 116 >>>>>

Equipment: 5 cones, 3 bibs and footballs
Number of players: 9
Dimensions: 12m x 5

The Game:

- The six players on the perimeter of the pentagon attempt to keep the ball.

- They are only allowed to move between the cones and cannot enter the pitch.

- A support player, on the inside, works with the perimeter players.

- Three defenders, on the inside, try to intercept the ball.

- If successful, they attempt to keep the ball away from the support player (3 v 1), but are only allowed one-touch passes.

- If they take more than one touch or they lose possession, then the ball is returned to the perimeter players and the game continues.

- Work for three minutes and then change the defenders and support players.

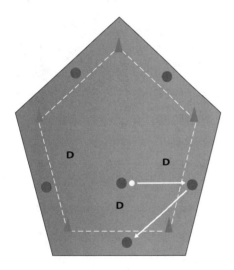

Exercise 117 >>>>>

Equipment: 6 cones, 2 sets of bibs and footballs
Number of players: 12
Dimensions: 20m x 6

The Game:

- The players are divided into two teams of six, each team in different coloured bibs.

- Three players from each team are placed at the six points of the hexagon (diagram 1) and act as support players for their team.

- The remaining players work inside the hexagon and play 3 v 3.

- If the attacking team complete six consecutive passes, they gain a point.

- Work for three minutes then change inside players.

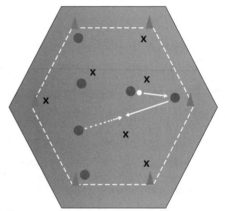

Variation

- The perimeter players stand on the sides of the hexagon (diagram 2).

- They may move up and down their side of the shape, but only between the cones.

- They cannot pass back to the player that gave them the ball.

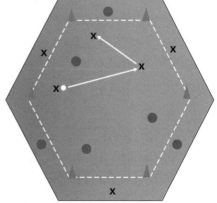

Progression

- Whoever passes to a support player, takes his place.

- This should encourage even greater movement.

Exercise 118 〉〉〉〉〉

| Equipment: 6 cones, 3 bibs and footballs |
| Number of players: 10 |
| Dimensions: 12m x 6 |

The Game:

- The six players on the perimeter of the hexagon attempt to keep the ball.

- They are only allowed to move between the cones and cannot enter the pitch.

- A support player, on the inside, works with the perimeter players.

- Three defenders, on the inside, try to intercept the ball.

- If successful, they attempt to keep the ball away from the support player (3 v 1) but are only allowed one-touch passes.

- If they take more than one touch or they lose possession, then the ball is returned to the perimeter players.

- Work for three minutes then change the defenders and support players.

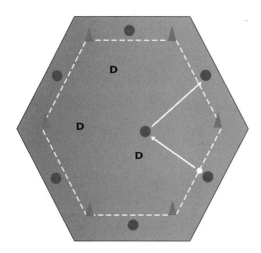

Exercise 119 〉〉〉〉〉

| Equipment: 8 cones, 2 footballs and 2 sets of bibs |
| Number of players: 12 to 18 |
| Dimensions: 3 x 25m x 20m grids |

The Game:

- A 60m x 25m grid is divided into three equal parts, as in the diagram.

- Two players from each team are placed in each grid.

- Both teams start with a ball and play through each other.

- Players are allowed to move grids but there must ALWAYS be two players per team in each grid.

- Therefore, if one player moves in, another must move out.

- Once players understand the concept, make the game competitive.

- Teams score one point for eight consecutive passes.

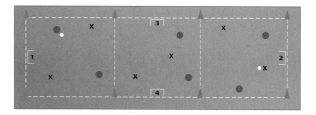

Progression One

- A goal (no. 1 and 2) is placed on each end line.

- Each team now has a goal to attack and a goal to defend.

- Teams can only score with a one-touch finish.

- As before, players may move from grid to grid, but there must always be two players from each team in each grid.

- Goals do not count if this rule is violated.

Progression Two

- A goal (no. 3 and 4) is placed on the centre of each sideline.

- The shape of the pitch now changes but teams still have one goal to attack and one to defend.

- Teams still score with a one-touch finish.

- Players may move from grid to grid but there can only be two players per team in each grid.

Training Cards

Training cards, with shapes, numbers or colours on them, can help develop field awareness. The cards are held up by the coach, as players perform skills with the ball or plyometric exercises such as hopping. For example, whilst dribbling a ball, players call out the shape, colour or number which is being held up. The task can be made harder if the coach moves around the grid.

Exercise 120 》》》》》

Equipment: 4 cones, 8 training cards and 12 balls

Number of players: 12

Dimensions: 20m x 20m grid

The Game:

- Players have a ball each and dribble anywhere in the grid.

- The coach has eight training cards, with the shape of a triangle, diagonal, square and circle and four numbers from 1 to 4.

- The coach holds up a shape or number and the players have to call out what is on the card, whilst maintaining control of their ball.

- The coach can make the task more difficult by moving around the grid.

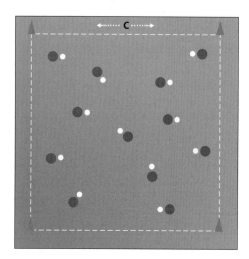

Variation

- Players juggle the ball on the move, whilst calling out the shape or number held up.

Exercise 121 》》》》》

Equipment: 4 cones, 8 training cards and 3 balls

Number of players: 12

Dimensions: 20m x 20m grid

The Game:

- Twelve players randomly pass three footballs amongst themselves whilst constantly moving.

- However, before passing the ball, they must call out the shape or number which the coach holds up.

- The coach can make their task harder by moving around the square.

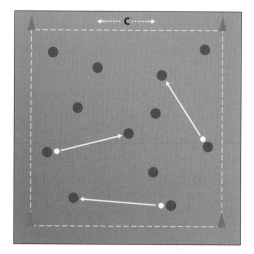

Progression

- To make the practice more demanding, players hop on one foot and pass with the other.

- The player with the ball calls out the shape, colour or number held up by the coach, before passing the ball.

- At no stage should he put his striking foot on the ground.

- The coach should keep changing the hopping leg, as this is a very demanding exercise.

Exercise 122 〉〉〉〉〉

Equipment: 4 cones, 8 training cards and 12 balls

Number of players: 12

Dimensions: 20m x 20m square

The Game:

- Players have a ball each and dribble anywhere in the square.

- The coach has four training cards with shapes of a triangle, diagonal, square and circle on them.

- He randomly holds up the shapes as the players are working.

- Each shape represents a different task for the players to perform. For example:

    Triangle: dribble with right foot only.

    Diagonal: dribble with left foot only.

    Square: roll the ball with soles of the feet.

    Circle: dribble with either foot.

- The coach should keep varying the action to be taken.

Variation

- The coach has four training cards with numbers 1 to 4 on them.

- Each number represents a different task for the players to perform. For example:

    1 = juggle with right foot only.

    2 = juggle with left foot only.

    3 = juggle using the thighs only.

    4 = juggle using the head.

- The coach should keep varying the action to be taken.

Progression

- The coach either holds up a shape or a number.

- The players therefore either dribble the ball or juggle the ball.

- The coach should quickly change the required action.

- The task can be made more difficult if the coach moves around the square.

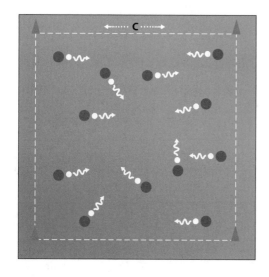

Exercise 123 〉〉〉〉〉

Equipment: 4 cones, 12 training cards and

3 footballs   Number of players: 12

Dimensions: 20m x 20m grid

The Game:

- Players randomly pass three footballs amongst themselves.

- When a rhythm has been established, they then broaden their vision by reacting to different training cards, which the coach holds up.

- Each shape represents a different task for the players to perform.

  Triangle: exchange the ball with a takeover.

  Diagonal: exchange the ball with a drag back.

  Square: play a one-two with another player.

  Circle: two-touch passing only.

- The aim is to raise the player's line of vision away from the ball.

- The coach should keep changing the response required from each shape.

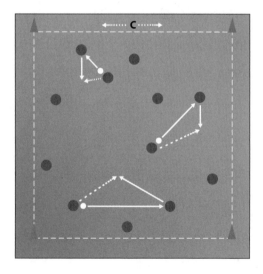

Progression One

- Each number represents a different task for the players to perform.

  1 = players pass with the outside of the foot only.

  2 = players pass with the right foot only.

  3 = players pass with their left foot only.

  4 = players pass with either foot.

- The coach should keep changing the response required from each number.

Progression Two

- Each coloured card represents a different task for the players to perform.

  Yellow: player heads the ball out of his own hands.

  Green: player volleys the ball out of his own hands.

  Blue: player volleys the ball from the thigh.

  Red: player throws the ball for the next player to control and catch.

Progression Three

- The coach combines any two from shape, number or colour.

The Reactor Bib with Symbols

It is only in the last 50 years that training methods have become far more innovative. However, there is still much to learn about how we train young players, what type of practices we use, what movement skills are taught and what coaching styles we employ. We know that players must start playing the game at between six and eight years of age and that many of the complicated motor skills required must be in place by the age of twelve.

It is therefore essential that we help young players become familiar with the ball and develop basic tactical understanding. However, we believe it is possible to take things even further and assist players to focus their attention on important cues, which, in turn, will lead to greater perception and faster decision-making. It is vital that we 'coach' the mind, the cognitive processes and intelligence, as well as technique.

With this in mind, we have developed the reactor bib with symbols. On one side of the bib there are shapes - rectangles, circles, diagonals and triangles - and on the other, numbers from one to four. Geometric shapes and numbers are already markings that children know from school so it is quite easy to transfer them to the football field. By using the bibs, players will be able to acquire and improve tactical elements of their game, as they will have to quickly adapt their actions to the problems they are presented with. In addition, peripheral vision will also be improved as the bibs will encourage players to move their focus from the ball to the target, at the moment of contact or even before. This will train the players to have a better feel for the ball, as they are less likely to look down at it. We believe the bibs have great educational potential thanks to the large number and variety of exercises that they can be used for.

We require attentive players, with good all-round vision and the ability to adapt quickly to changes of pace and shape. The bibs will help achieve this, with the coach suggesting various geometric shapes to be formed such as a triangle, diagonal, circle, or rectangle, all of which are tactical formations found in the game and which will help players understand the concept of shape and distance.

When this has been understood, the coach will then progress to players passing from one shape to another, or one number to another, in a pre-arranged sequence. In addition, since communication is so essential to any teaching or learning process, players will call out the shape or number they are passing to or shape or number they have received from. For more advanced players, encourage them to call out the shape or number they are going to pass to BEFORE they receive the ball.

We have devised a programme of activities and invasion games to be used with this training aid, which will help the coach get the most out of this new and original idea. We are confident that, with a little imagination, coaches will be able to come up with their own ideas and practices.

Activities using the Reactor Bibs

Key:				
	△	□	x	○
Shapes	Triangle	Rectangle	Diagonal	Circle
Numbers	1	2	3	4
Colours	Red	Yellow	Blue	Green

Exercise 124 ⟫⟫⟫⟫

Equipment: 4 cones, 16 reactor bibs and 16 balls

Number of players: 16

Dimensions: 30m x 30m square

The Game:

- Four teams of four players are positioned in the square.

- Each player has a ball and each team wears a different shaped bib.

- Players start by carrying the ball and sprinting, twisting and turning anywhere in the grid, looking to attack space.

- Every so often the coach calls out one of the shapes eg 'circles tag'.

- The circles then become the chasers and try to tag the other three shapes, by touching them with their balls. The chasers cannot throw their balls.

- Every time a player is caught, he has to stand with the ball above the head and legs apart.

- The only way a player can be freed is if one of the players being chased rolls a ball through his legs.

- After one minute, the game is stopped and players go back to running in the grid and attacking space, until the coach calls out another shape.

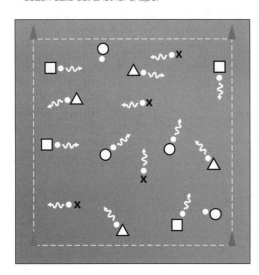

Progression One

- As above but players can only be freed by one of their own shapes e.g. if a diagonal is caught, they can only be freed by a diagonal.

- Can the chasers tag all the members of one team?

Progression Two

- The ball is now placed on the ground and dribbled.

- As before, any player caught can only be freed if the ball is passed through his legs by a player of the same shape.

Exercise 125 ⟫⟫⟫⟫

Equipment: 4 cones, 16 reactor bibs and 4 balls

Number of players: 16

Dimensions: 30m x 30m square

The Game:

- Four balls are passed randomly amongst the group.

- Players then pass in the order designated by the coach eg triangle to diagonal, to circle, to rectangle and back to triangle.

- The coach should keep changing the combinations in order to make the players think.

- Numbers or colours could be used instead of shapes.

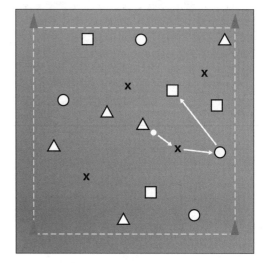

Progression

- Players pass in order, but follow their pass and close the receiver down.

- Instead of passes, players exchange the ball by take-overs.

Exercise 126 ⟩⟩⟩⟩⟩

Equipment: 4 cones, 16 reactor bibs and 4 balls

Number of players: 16

Dimensions: 30m x 25m grid

The Game:

- Four balls are passed randomly amongst the four shapes.

- As players pass the ball, they call out the shape they are passing to.

- When a pattern has been established, encourage the receiver to call out the shape he has received from.

- Numbers or colours could be used instead of shapes.

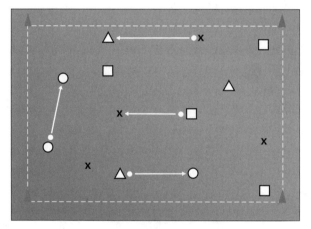

Progression One

- One shape passes to his own shape, gets the ball back (set up play) then passes to a different shape e.g. a triangle passes to a triangle, gets the ball back, then passes to a rectangle and the process starts again.

- The above exercise could be used with numbers or colours.

Progression Two

- Play 12 v 4. As the attackers pass the ball, they have to call out the shape they are passing to.

- For experienced players, make them call out the name of the shape they are going to pass to BEFORE receiving the ball.

Exercise 127 ⟩⟩⟩⟩⟩

Equipment: 4 cones, 16 reactor bibs and 3-4 balls

Number of players: 16

Dimensions: 25m x 20m grid

The Game:

- 12 v 4. Circles defend against the other three shapes.

- The attacking players are restricted to two touches.

- After passing the ball, the attacking player has to sprint to the nearest touchline before he can rejoin the game.

- Change the defending shape every five minutes.

- Numbers or colours could be used instead of shapes.

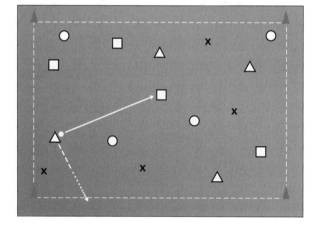

Progression

- The attacking team has to pass in the order designated by the coach eg rectangle to diagonal, to triangle and back to rectangle.

- This is a difficult exercise, so only experienced players should sprint to the nearest touchline after passing the ball.

- Less experienced players simply sprint out of the space after passing the ball.

Exercise 128 ⟫⟫⟫

Equipment: 4 cones, 16 reactor bibs and
several footballs   Number of players: 16
Dimensions: half a pitch

The Game:

- 8 v 8. Numbers 1 and 3 play against numbers 2 and 4.

- Teams attempt to keep possession and a point is awarded for eight consecutive passes.

- Keep changing the combination, so that players have to think.

- Shapes or colours could be used instead of numbers.

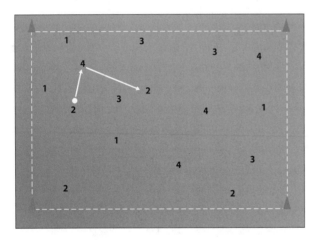

Progression

- As above but teams have to pass alternately when in possession eg 1 to 3 and back to 1 or 2 to 4 and back to 2. This exercise should only be used with more advanced players.

Exercise 129 ⟫⟫⟫

Equipment: 4 cones, 16 reactor bibs, 4 goals
and several footballs   Number of players: 16
Dimensions: 40m x 40m square

The Game:

- Play two games of 4 v 4 plus four goalkeepers.

- A goal is placed in the centre of each touchline, with red bibs playing against green bibs and blue bibs playing against yellow bibs, as in the diagram.

- If there are no goalkeepers, shots or throws only count if the ball hits a cone placed in the centre of the goal.

- All four teams play at the same time, with two games going on simultaneously.

- With two balls and sixteen players working in the same area, space is very limited.

- Change opponents every 10 minutes.

- Numbers or shapes could be used instead of colours.

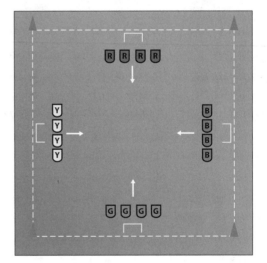

Progression

- Play a game with red and green combining to make one team and blue and yellow combining to make another.

- Each team has two goals to defend and two to attack.

- Different restrictions could be placed on each team eg red and blue two touches, green and yellow three touches.

Exercise 130 ⟫⟫⟫

Equipment: 4 cones, 16 reactor bibs and 4 balls

Number of players: 16

Dimensions: 40m x 30m grid

The Game:

- Four balls are passed randomly amongst the group.

- However, players CANNOT pass to the shape the ball was received from.

- Therefore, if a circle receives from a triangle, the ball has to be passed to a shape other than a triangle.

- This will make players concentrate, improve their vision and force the correct body shape.

- Numbers or colours could be used instead of shapes.

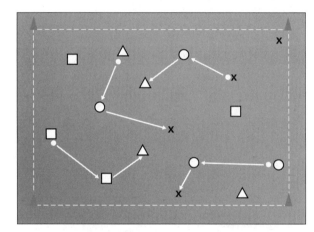

Progression

- Play 12 v 4.

- The attacking players CANNOT pass to a shape they received the ball from. This will immediately cut the number of passing options.

Exercise 131 ⟫⟫⟫

Equipment: 4 cones, 16 reactor bibs and 4 balls

Number of players: 16

Dimensions: 40m x 30m grid

The Game:

- Four balls are passed randomly amongst the group.

- However, each group is assigned a number it CANNOT pass to.

- For example, 1 cannot pass to 4, 4 cannot pass to 3, 3 cannot pass to 2 and 2 cannot pass to 1.

- In order to maintain concentration, the coach should keep changing the number a team cannot pass to.

- Colours or shapes could be used instead of numbers.

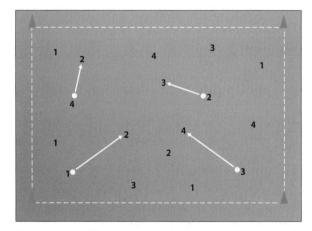

Progression

- Play 12 v 4.

- Each team is assigned a number it cannot pass to.

- The defending team is missed out in the sequence.

- For example, if 2's are the defenders, 1's cannot pass to 4, 4's cannot pass to 3 and 3's cannot pass to 1.

- This will cut the number of passing options for the attacking players.

- The coach should change the forbidden number every time the defenders change.

Exercise 132 >>>>>

Equipment: 4 cones, 16 reactor bibs and footballs

Number of players: 16

Dimensions: 40m x 30m grid

The Game:

- Play 8 v 8 keep ball. Triangles and diagonals combine to play against circles and rectangles.

- However, triangles and circles are limited to two touches but diagonals and rectangles play without restrictions.

- Award one point for eight consecutive passes.

- For more advanced players, restrict triangles and circles to one touch and diagonals and rectangles to three touches.

- Colours or numbers could be used instead of shapes.

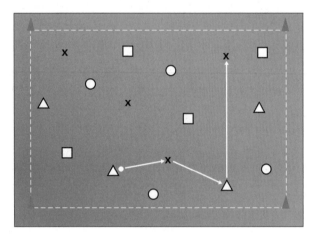

Progression One

- There is no restriction on the number of touches but triangles and circles are limited to passes under 10 metres, whilst diagonals and rectangles must pass over 10 metres.

Progression Two

- Play 12 v 4, with circles acting as defenders.

- Diagonals are restricted to one touch, rectangles to two touches and triangles to three touches.

Exercise 133 >>>>>

Equipment: 4 cones, 16 reactor bibs and 4 balls

Number of players: 16

Dimensions: 30m x 30m square

The Game:

- All four groups start off in the square, with one ball per team.

- The players in each group are numbered from 1 to 4.

- Number 1 starts with the ball and passes to number 2, number 2 passes to number 3, number 3 passes to number 4 and number 4 passes back to number 1.

- Players have unlimited touches of the ball.

- When a rhythm has been established, add a second ball. Numbers 1 and 3 start with the balls.

- Colours or numbers could be used instead of shapes.

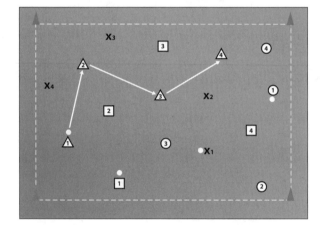

Progression One

- Once the last player is reached, pass in reverse order e.g. 1 2 3 4 3 2 1.

Progression Two

- Number 1 does not pass to number 2 until he calls for the ball. Number 2 does not pass to number 3 until he calls for the ball and so on.

- This will force the player with the ball to keep his head up and observe carefully the player he is going to pass to.

Progression Three

- Number 1 dribbles the ball at pace for 3/4 seconds, then leaves it for number 2 to pick up. Number 2 then does the same for number 3 and so on.

- This will force the player without the ball to observe the dribbler carefully and then react explosively when the ball is left.

Exercise 134 》》》》》

Equipment: 4 cones, 16 reactor bibs and 3 balls

Number of players: 16

Dimensions: 30m x 30m square

The Game:

- Circles, triangles and diagonals start off in the square; rectangles are placed on the perimeter and act as wall passers.

- Rectangles are limited to two touches and may move up and down their side of the square.

- Each group has a ball.

- Players of each group in the square are numbered from 1 to 4.

- Number 1 starts with the ball and plays a 'give and go' with any rectangle, before passing to number 2.

- Number 2 wall passes with a NEW rectangle before passing to number 3 and so on.

- Good communication is vital. Players must call out the name of the outside player they are passing to, whilst the outside player should do the same when returning the ball.

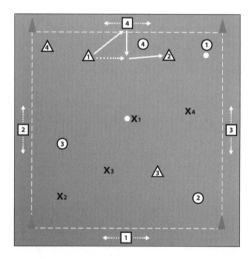

Progression One

- As above except the player with the ball has the choice of passing to the next numbered player in the sequence (1 to 2, 2 to 3 etc) **OR** passing to a perimeter player and getting the ball back.

Progression Two

- As above, except the perimeter player has to pass back to the **NEXT** player in the sequence, not the player who gave him the ball. Therefore, if triangle 1 passes to a perimeter player, the perimeter player has to pass back to triangle 2. Much greater visual awareness and communication are now required.

Progression Three

- Play 8 v 4 keep ball, with one group acting as defenders.
- The attacking players may use any of the perimeter players for a wall pass.

Progression Four

- As above, except the perimeter players **CANNOT** pass back to the player who gave them the ball, but must pass to a player wearing the same shape.

Exercise 135 》》》》》

Equipment: 4 cones, 16 reactor bibs and 4 balls

Number of players: 16

Dimensions: 40m x 30m grid

The Game:

- Four teams of four players are positioned on the field, with one ball per team.

- Each team passes to its own players and attempts to find free spaces.

- Encourage players to be creative. Look for wall passes, takeovers, overlaps, double passes, double passes involving a third person etc.

- When a rhythm has been established, allow players to pass to a different number, but that player has to return the ball first time (one-touch play).

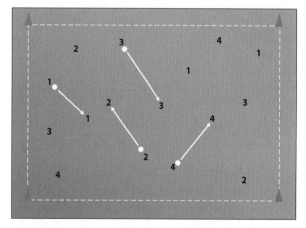

Progression One

- On a signal from the coach, the players sprint in four different directions, so that each team is gathered in a different corner of the field.

- Here they continue to pass the ball until the coach gives the signal to return to the field.

- As above, but four players of four **different** numbers sprint to each corner of the field and carry on passing the ball.

Progression Two

- Teams 1 and 3 combine to play against teams 2 and 4.
- One point is awarded for six consecutive passes.
- However, there are different ball possession rules for the teams.
- Teams 1 and 2 have to pass the ball first time, whilst teams 3 and 4 are not restricted and may dribble before passing.
- Keep changing the ball possession rules for the teams.

Equipment: 4 cones, 16 reactor bibs and 4 balls

Number of players: 16

Dimensions: 40m x 40m square

The Game:

- Four teams of four players are positioned in the square, with one ball per team.

- Each team passes to its own players, whilst attempting to occupy free space.

- The aim is to work on combination plays, without interfering with the other teams in the square.

- Encourage players to look for wall passes, takeovers, overlaps and double passes.

- Colours or numbers could be used instead of shapes or a combination of each.

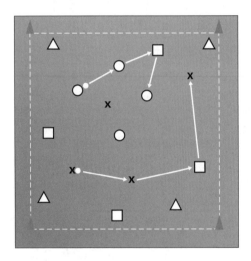

Progression One

- Two shapes (in this case triangles and rectangles) act as support players on the perimeter of the square.

- Circles and diagonals continue to work on combination plays, but now include overlaps, wall passes, takeovers and double passes with the perimeter players as well.

- Work for three minutes, then change with the perimeter players.

Progression Two

- 4 v 4 keep ball, circles v diagonals.

- The inside players look for combinations with their own team and also look for wall passes, overlaps and double passes with the perimeter players.

- The perimeter players cannot be tackled and must always return the ball to the team they received the pass from.

Progression Three

- Combine two shapes e.g. triangles with diagonals and rectangles with circles.

- The two teams on the inside (in this case, circles and diagonals) can only make wall passes, overlaps or double passes with their support team on the perimeter of the square.

- To make the game more dynamic, when a player from the centre passes to a perimeter player and shouts 'change', the perimeter player dribbles into the square and changes places with the passer.

- This could mean all four shapes operating inside the square at any one time and so visual awareness and communication now become even more vital.

Exercise 137 ⟩⟩⟩⟩⟩

Equipment: 4 cones, 16 reactor bibs and 4 balls

Number of players: 16

Dimensions: 40m x 30m grid

The Game:

- Two teams of eight players are positioned on the pitch, with two balls per team.

- Odd numbers (1s and 3s) and circles and diagonals work together as one team and even numbers (2s and 4s) and triangles and rectangles work together as another.

- The teams start off passing both balls by hand and play through each other.

- When a rhythm has been established, change to passing both balls by feet.

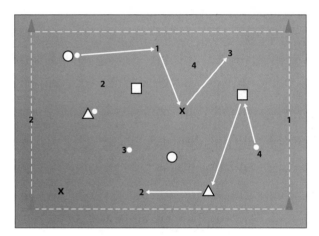

Progression One

- Pass one ball by hand and one ball by feet.

- This will ensure that players have to move their heads from high to low and vice versa.

- Players then pass in sequence eg number to shape and back to number but still move one ball by hand and the other by feet.

Progression Two

- Play 8 v 8 keep ball - odd numbers and circles and diagonals versus even numbers and triangles and rectangles.

- Teams pass by hand and score one point for eight consecutive passes.

- When a rhythm has been established, make players pass in sequence e.g. number to shape and back to number.

- This will halve the number of passing options and make players work much harder off the ball.

Progression Three

- The ball is now passed along the ground.

- A point is awarded for eight consecutive passes.

- When a rhythm has been established, make players pass in sequence eg numbers to shapes, back to numbers.

Progression Four

- Work with two balls - one is passed by hand, the other is passed by feet.

- One team starts with both balls.

- The ball passed by hand could be of a different colour or shape to the one passed by feet.

- This game will require great peripheral vision as players will have to focus on one ball whilst being aware of the position of the other.

- Can one team keep possession of both balls?

Goalkeeping

The goalkeeper's job gives him a unique position in the team. He therefore needs a special training programme to prepare him for his specific role. However, this must be more than the usual individual training and 'busy' activities endured by most goalkeepers today. They are part of a team, so they need a lot of game-orientated exercises, where there is contact with their own teammates. The biggest criticism of most goalkeeping training is that it isn't game-orientated enough. If goalkeepers don't face realistic situations in practice, how are they going to develop the required skills when dealing with these situations in a game? It is vital that goalkeepers are part of a team and not apart from a team! There will be many occasions when goalkeepers practise on their own, with their specialised trainer, but they must also be integrated into the majority of most sessions. By reacting to the movements of the ball and opponents in match situations, the goalkeeper will get a better understanding of the game. Not only will this improve his field skills, it will also help team solidarity and team spirit.

Goalkeepers must develop good training habits, since they are likely to be tested a lot more in practice than in a game. It is essential that they are not lazy or lack concentration during training, as they will miss out on their best opportunity to improve. Success depends on preparation, so to achieve a high level of performance, the goalkeeper must commit totally to training.

The best goalkeepers are always consistent in their decision-making. For example, they will know when to come for a cross and when to hold their line. Their favourable position on the field gives them a good overview of the whole playing area. They are therefore able to support their teammates, particularly in organising the defence or directing players if they are on the wrong side of attackers. Communication is therefore essential, particularly the tone of voice, which must suggest urgency but not panic.

Due to the change in the back pass law, the modern goalkeeper has to be more than just a shot stopper. He must be able to receive difficult bouncing balls with either foot or other permitted body parts and to pass accurately with the left or right foot. In fact, the goalkeeper needs most of the skills required by outfield players, so should be encouraged to take part as an outfield player in 5 a-side games.

The goalkeeping training has been divided into the following sections:

- Shot stopping
- Crossing
- Distribution
- Dealing with the back pass
- Communication

Each section provides goalkeeping exercises which optimise the use of visual information and develop perceptual skills. The goalkeepers will always be put in situations which require a shift of attention from the ball to the surrounding environment. The exercises are progressive and will eventually be combined, so that shot stopping, crossing and dealing with the back pass will always conclude with distribution. The exercises combine the technical, tactical, psychological and physical, which are the 'four pillars' of the game as far as goalkeepers are concerned. The exercises will also enable the coach to assess a goalkeeper and track the amount of progress made in his development, as well as show up areas of weakness.

Goalkeeping
>>>>>>
Shot Stopping

Exercise 138 >>>>>>

Equipment: 2 coloured poles and footballs

Number of players: 2

The Game:

- The goalkeeper stands between two coloured poles/cones which are 4 metres apart.

- A server, who is holding a ball, calls the colour of one of the poles, which the goalkeeper has to touch.

- The server then plays the ball along the ground towards the opposite pole.

- The keeper has to change direction quickly and dive to save.

- The aim of the practice is to ensure that the keeper takes off from the correct foot.

- For example, when diving to the right he MUST take off from the right foot and when diving to the left, he MUST take off from the left foot.

- The action is repeated six times and then the players change roles.

Progression One

- Vary the service from low, to waist and then above head height.

Exercise 139 >>>>>>

Equipment: 4 coloured poles/cones and footballs

Number of players: 4 (1 worker and 3 servers)

The Game:

- The keeper starts off in the goal, as indicated by the diagram.

- Server 1 feeds him the ball, which he catches and returns immediately.

- Server 1 then calls the colour of the next goal, which the keeper has to enter.

- For example, if he calls out "blue", server 2 will strike the ball into the blue goal, for the goalkeeper to save.

- The ball is returned to server 2.

- The keeper immediately returns to the starting goal to face server 1 and the process starts again.

- The action is repeated six times and then the players change roles.

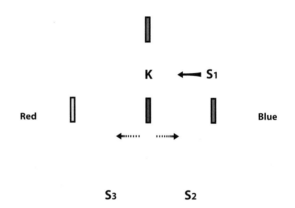

Progression One

- Instead of calling out a colour, server 1 calls out a number e.g 1 or 2.

- The keeper immediately sprints to the numbered goal called out.

Progression Two

- Combine the above so that server 1 either calls out a colour or number eg red or 2, blue or 1.

Progression Three

- If server 1 calls out "blue", the keeper enters that goal.

- However the ball is fed by the opposite server, in this example server 3.

Exercise 140 》》》》》

Equipment: 6 poles (inc 1 red, 1 green, 1 blue and 1 yellow) and footballs

Number of players: 6 (1 worker, 5 servers)

The Game:

- Four goals are set up, as in the diagram.

- They are given a colour (yellow, blue, green, red).

- Server O starts by playing the ball for the keeper to catch and return.

- Server O immediately calls out the colour of a goal, which the keeper has to enter.

- For example, if he calls out green, the keeper has to sprint to the green goal.

- Server 3 immediately plays him a ball, which the keeper attempts to save.

- He then sprints back to his original starting position and receives another pass and instruction from server O.

- The action is repeated six times and then players change roles.

Progression One

- The goals are changed from colours to numbers.

Progression Two

- Combine colours and numbers.

Progression Three

- Add another server (server 5), as in the diagram.

- The practice now starts with either server O or server 5.

- They work alternately to start with, but then allow them to work randomly.

Exercise 141 》》》》》

Equipment: 6 cones, 2 goals, 2 sets of bibs and a supply of footballs Number of players: 8+2 keepers

Dimensions: 36m x 40m

The Game:

- Play 4 v 4 on a pitch twice the size of the penalty area.

- Use the edge of the penalty area as the half-way line.

- Play a normal game of football, but encourage players to shoot at every opportunity.

- At the start, players may only shoot from the defensive half of the field.

- To encourage a high tempo, spare footballs should be placed around the outside of the pitch and in each goal.

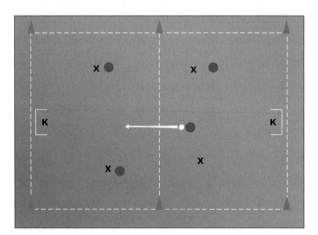

Progression One

- Players may only shoot from the attacking half of the field.

Progression Two

- Players must shoot from alternate parts of the pitch.

- For example, if the first shot is from the attacking half, the next must be from the defensive half.

- This represents shots from inside and outside the penalty area, which is realistic to the game.

Progression Three

- Remove all restrictions and allow players to shoot from anywhere.

Goalkeeping
>>>>>
Crossing

Before training goalkeepers to deal with crosses, it is essential that they are taught how to jump correctly using three small steps. The reasons for this are:

- Too many goalkeepers try to take off after a big lunge. In this extended position, it is difficult to change direction.

- The long step creates a weak position, with lots of force going forwards which then has to be transferred upwards. Massive leg strength is required to achieve this.

- Muscles are in an exaggerated, elongated position, so they cannot create much contractile force.

- All the weight is on the front foot. If the foot slips or the ground is slippery, take off will be poor.

Exercise 142 >>>>>>

Equipment: 3 cones or markers
Number of players: 1

The Game:

- Three cones are laid out in a line, about a foot apart. This distance can be adjusted according to the age and size of the player.

- The goalkeeper starts behind the first cone.

- Whichever foot he leads with will be the foot he takes off from.

- In the diagram below, he steps forward onto his left foot, takes a short step with his right foot and takes off on his left foot.

- It is essential that he takes off on the third step, with the centre of gravity over his left leg and not behind it. This will help generate greater upward force and allow the keeper more control over his movement.

- The action should be repeated 10 times, with the coach correcting any obvious mistakes.

Exercise 143 >>>>>>

Equipment: 8 footballs (2 red, 2 blue, 2 yellow and 2 green), 4 bibs (colours as balls) and 1 goal
Number of players: 8 (4 goalkeepers and 4 servers)

The Game:

- Each goalkeeper is allocated a ball and bib of the same colour.

- Each server holds a ball of a different colour.

- The balls are served one at a time but in any order.

- The goalkeepers only catch the coloured ball they have been allocated.

- The game should be played at a high tempo. As soon as one ball has been served, the next should be on its way.

- Once the server has thrown his ball, he quickly picks up the second ball ready to throw.

- When all the balls have been served, the two groups change roles.

- Both groups have three goes and then the action is repeated from the opposite side.

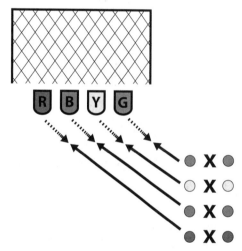

Progression

- The footballs are placed in a pool and can now be picked up and crossed by **any** server.

- Balls are still thrown one at a time, but the goalkeeper will now be uncertain which server he is going to receive from.

Exercise 144 >>>>>>

Equipment: 8 footballs (2 red, 2 blue, 2 yellow and 2 green), 4 bibs (colours as balls) and 1 goal

Number of players: 8 (4 goalkeepers and 4 servers)

The Game:

- Each goalkeeper is given a coloured bib to wear, but is allocated a **different** coloured ball to catch.

- For example, the red goalkeeper attacks the blue ball, the blue goalkeeper the yellow ball, the yellow goalkeeper the green ball and the green goalkeeper, the red ball.

- The footballs should be served one at a time, but as soon as one ball is caught, the next should be on its way.

- It is essential that a high tempo is maintained.

- When all the footballs have been served, the two groups change roles.

- Both groups have three goes and then the action is repeated from the opposite side.

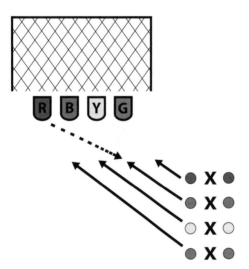

Progression

- Only two servers are used.

- They randomly pick up balls from the pool and serve them one at a time.

- At the same time, the goalkeepers are given a different coloured ball to catch. This will force them to concentrate.

Exercise 145 >>>>>>

Equipment: 8 footballs (2 red, 2 blue, 2 yellow and 2 green), 4 bibs (colours as balls) and 1 goal

Number of players: 8 (4 goalkeepers and 4 servers)

The Game:

- Each server holds a different coloured ball.

- All four footballs are delivered simultaneously.

- Each goalkeeper has to identify his coloured ball and then attack it.

- This makes the game more realistic, as each goalkeeper has to concentrate on his ball and not be put off by those around him.

- This equates to a crowded penalty area.

- When all the balls have been served, the two groups change roles.

- Both groups have three goes each and then the action is repeated from the opposite side.

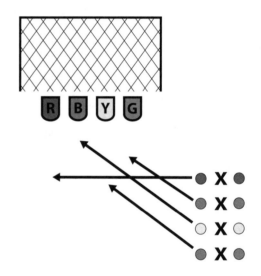

Progression One

- The goalkeepers start by closing their eyes.

- They only open them on a call from the coach.

Progression Two

- The goalkeepers stand facing the field but look away from the servers.

- On a signal from the coach, the players turn and react to their ball.

Exercise 146 ⟫⟫⟫

Equipment: 8 cones, 1 set of bibs and footballs

Number of players: 5 v 5 + 2 keepers

Dimensions: 36 x 44 yards + 2 36 x 5 yards channels

The Game:

- Two teams play 3 v 3 on a pitch 36m x 44m plus two crossing channels.

- Two servers are placed in each crossing channel.

- The game starts with one of the goalkeepers, who passes into one of the crossing channels.

- A server can either cross the ball or set it for the other server to cross.

- The emphasis must be on the goalkeepers, who have to communicate with their defence and organise the defenders.

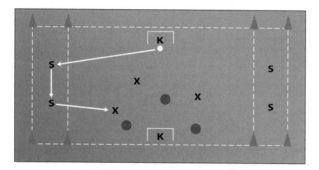

Progression One

- Only the outfield players can pass to the servers.

- The goalkeepers pass to outfield players but not servers.

Progression Two

- A normal game, but two servers work for one team and two for the other.

- The servers cannot tackle each other.

Progression Three

- Play 5 v 5 plus two goalkeepers.

- An attacking player can move into a channel and cross the ball, without opposition.

Exercise 147 ⟫⟫⟫

Equipment: 12 cones, 5 coloured balls and

5 white balls

Number of players: 4

The Game:

- Three squares are marked out as in the diagram below.

- Goalkeeper R1 and goalkeeper R2 each stand in a separate square and act as full backs.

- The server plays the ball to the goalkeeper, with varied service.

- If the goalkeeper saves a white football, then he must open out to the left and pass or throw to player R2.

- If the goalkeeper saves a coloured football, then he must open out to the right and pass or throw to player R1.

- Work for 10 reps, then change roles.

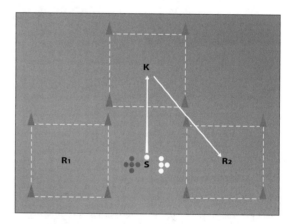

Progression

- If a coloured ball is served, the goalkeeper has to pick it up and throw.

- If a white ball is served, the goalkeeper has to control it with his feet and pass.

- As he serves, the feeder calls out 2 or 3 and the goalkeeper has to pass or throw to that player.

Equipment: 1 goal, 8 cones, 10 footballs

(5 white and 5 coloured)

Number of players: 4

The Game:

- Two squares (R2 and R3) are marked out on the corners of the penalty area and a receiver is placed in each square.

- The server, with 10 footballs, stands on the edge of the penalty area and volleys a shot at the goalkeeper.

- The goalkeeper saves and if it's a coloured ball, distributes quickly to R2.

- If it's a white ball, he distributes to R3.

- Repeat 10 times, then change roles.

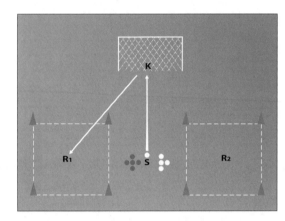

Progression One

- As above, but the receivers start **outside** their square.

- The goalkeeper now passes or throws the ball into the appropriate square for the receiver to run onto.

Progression Two

- The receiver can start inside the square or outside.

- The goalkeeper now has to choose the appropriate pass, either into feet or into space, for the receiver to run onto.

Equipment: 10 footballs, 1 goal, 16 cones and

4 bibs each of a different colour

Number of players: 6

The Game:

- The four receivers, each wearing a different coloured bib, stand in the four squares, as in the diagram.

- The server, with 10 footballs, stands on the edge of the penalty area.

- He plays the ball to the goalkeeper and calls out a colour.

- The goalkeeper has to distribute the ball to that colour.

- It is essential that the goalkeeper works at a high tempo.

- As soon as he has saved the ball, he must get up and distribute it quickly.

- Once he has distributed the ball, the next one should be on its way from the server.

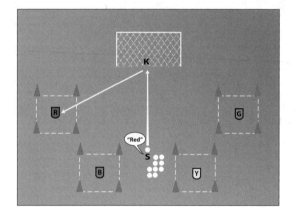

Progression One

- As before but the receivers stand outside their squares.

- The goalkeeper now has to throw or pass into space instead of feet.

Progression Two

- The receivers now have the choice of starting outside or inside the squares.

- This dictates whether the goalkeeper passes to feet or into space.

Exercise 150 ⟫⟫⟫

Equipment: 16 cones and 10 footballs

Number of players: 6 (1 keeper, 1 server and 4 receivers)

The Game:

- The server plays a ball for the goalkeeper to save.

- The four receivers may either stand inside the squares or outside, as in the diagram.

- If the receiver stands inside the square, he is an option and is free to receive the ball.

- If he is outside the square, he is **not** an option. This means that, for the purpose of the practice, he is marked, so cannot receive the ball.

- If there are two receivers inside a square, the goalkeeper has a choice of who he plays to.

- Repeat 10 times, then change roles.

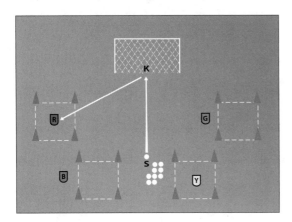

Progression

- The four receivers stand in the squares.

- However, any receiver with his back to the goalkeeper is not an option.

- Therefore, the goalkeeper can only pass the ball to a receiver facing him.

- If all four receivers have their back to the goalkeeper, then he must stay with the ball.

Exercise 151 ⟫⟫⟫

Equipment: 2 goals, 1 set of bibs, 16 cones and footballs **Number of players: 10 + 2 keepers**

Dimensions: 44m x 50m + 4 x 10 metre squares

The Game:

- A pitch 44 metres wide and 50 metres long is marked out as in the diagram.

- 4 x 10m squares are marked out within the pitch.

- When a goalkeeper has the ball, any of his players may enter a square.

- The goalkeeper may either pass to his player in the square or pass into the square for the player to run on to.

- The receiving player cannot be tackled whilst in the square.

- The game now becomes live.

- The goalkeeper does not have to serve into a square. He has the choice of distributing into the square or to a player anywhere on the field.

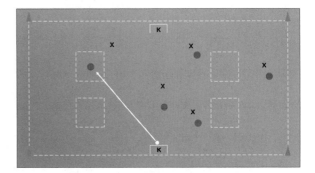

Progression

- The squares are then taken away.

- The same runs should still be made by the attacking players.

Goalkeeping

>>>>>

Dealing with the back pass

Exercise 152 >>>>>>

Equipment: 12 footballs (6 coloured, 6 white)
2 x 6 a-side goals with nets
Number of players: 2

The Game:

- The server plays the ball into the goalkeeper, as a back pass.

- The service can be varied, in order to replicate a game.

- The goalkeeper has to deal with the ball without using his hands.

- If the goalkeeper receives a white ball, he has to control it and pass it into the white goal.

- If he receives a coloured ball, he has to control it and pass it into the coloured goal.

- He therefore has to make a decision **before** the ball arrives.

- As soon as the goalkeeper has dealt with one ball, the next should be played in.

- Use all the footballs and then change roles.

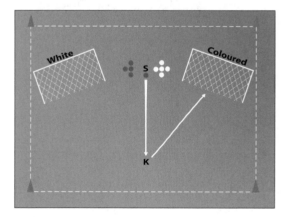

Progression One

- The server calls out the number of touches the goalkeeper is allowed, before passing into the correct goal e.g. one touch, three touches etc.

Progression Two

- The server plays a ball in to the goalkeeper.

- If it's a white ball, the keeper has to pass it into the coloured goal and if it's a coloured ball, into the white goal.

Progression Three

- The above practices are combined.

- The server calls out the number of touches and the goalkeeper then has to pass the coloured ball into the white goal and the white ball into the coloured goal.

Exercise 153 >>>>>>

Equipment: 4 cones, 1 goal, a set of bibs and
several footballs
Number of players: 9

The Game:

- A 12 metre square is marked out in front of the penalty area.

- Eight players work in the square, as in the diagram.

- The four players wearing bibs (X's) represent defenders.

- The four players without bibs (O's) represent attackers.

- The eight players start off randomly passing one ball to each other at a high tempo.

- At a signal from the coach, the player with the ball passes into the goalkeeper.

- If it is a defender (X), the goalkeeper has to identify this quickly and treat it as a back pass.

- He reacts by kicking the ball clear.

- If it is an attacker (O), he treats it as a shot, picks the ball up and throws it to the coach or designated target.

- The coach passes the next ball into the group of eight as quickly as possible and the action is repeated.

- After 10 attempts, change the goalkeeper.

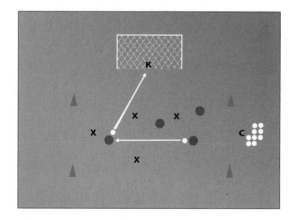

Exercise 154 ⟩⟩⟩⟩⟩

Equipment: 4 cones, 1 goal, set of bibs and balls

Number of players: 9

The Game:

- A 12 metre square is marked out in front of the penalty area.

- Eight players work in the square, as in the diagram.

- The four players wearing bibs (X's) are defenders.

- The four players without bibs (O's) are attackers.

- The eight players start off randomly passing a ball to each other, at a high tempo.

- At a signal from the coach, the player with the ball passes to the goalkeeper.

- If it's a defender, it is treated as a back pass.

- After passing the ball, the defender breaks out of the square and receives a pass from the goalkeeper.

- If a forward has a ball, he breaks out from the square and has a shot.

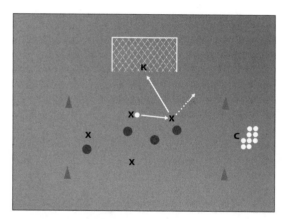

Progression One

- If a defender passes back, he immediately breaks out of the square to receive a pass from the goalkeeper.

- However, a forward chases down the back pass in order to make the goalkeeper's pass much more difficult.

Progression Two

- Once the ball has been passed back by the defender and is closed down by a forward, two defenders break out of the square to become options to receive the ball.

- One defender must break out from the top of the square and the other from the side.

- The goalkeeper now has a choice of which defender he passes to.

Once one ball is dead, it is essential that the next ball is fed in quickly by the coach, in order to maintain a high tempo.

Goalkeeping
⟩⟩⟩⟩⟩
Small-sided games for older players

Exercise 155 ⟩⟩⟩⟩⟩

Equipment: 2 goals, 4 cones, a set of bibs

Number of players: 8 + 2 goalkeepers

Dimensions: 40m x 30m

The Game:

- Both goalkeepers start as outfield players and can only use their feet.

- An outfield player from each team starts in goal.

- The aim is to help the outfield players appreciate the importance of a quality back pass.

- Each outfield player takes a turn in goal for three minutes.

- This small-sided game will last for 12 minutes.

- Players now resume their normal positions.

- A normal game is played except a goal can only be scored when the move has contained a back pass to the goalkeeper.

- The aim is to improve the goalkeeper's feet and give him confidence to deal with back passes.

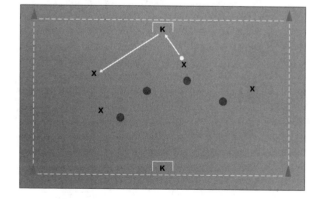

Exercise 156 〉〉〉〉〉

Equipment: 8 cones, 2 goals, balls and a set of bibs

Number of players: 6 + 2 goalkeepers

Dimensions: 30m x 25m

The Game:

- Both goalkeepers start as outfield players and can only use their feet.

- An outfield player from each team starts in goal.

- The aim is to help the outfield players appreciate the importance of a quality back pass.

- To help all the younger players, a safety zone is marked out in front of the goals, at each end of the pitch.

- Any back pass, into the safety zone to the goalkeeper, is unopposed.

- If an outfield player receives the ball in the safety zone, the game is live and he can still be challenged.

- Each outfield player takes a turn in goal for three minutes.

- This small-sided game will last for nine minutes.

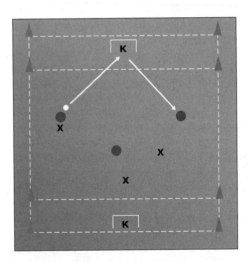

Progression One

- The goalkeepers now resume their normal positions.

- A goal can only be scored after an unopposed back pass to the goalkeeper.

- Both goalkeepers can still use their safety zone.

Progression Two

- As above, but the safety zone is taken away.

Goalkeeping
>>>>>
Communication

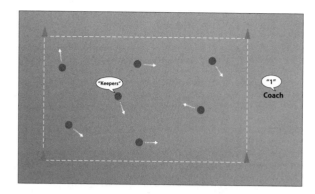

One of the priorities of any goalkeeper is to understand the basic principles of defending, as only then can he perform his role as coach on the field. The quality of the instructions given by a goalkeeper is just as important as any saves he makes, since he is the only person who can see the entire field and the other 21 players. As well as keeping his defence organized, the goalkeeper must also pay attention to what is happening off the ball, particularly on the weak side of defence. The proper positioning and body shape of defenders are essential, in order that attackers do not get blind side. It is the goalkeeper's job to ensure this does not happen.

As an attack gets closer to the goal, the gaps between defenders must get smaller and smaller, in order to prevent penetration. It is partly the goalkeeper's responsibility to make sure that all the attacking team's moves are played in front of or around the defence and not through it. This continuous communication with teammates will also aid concentration and add to the goalkeeper's presence in the team.

Exercise 157 >>>>>>

Equipment: 4 cones, Tach Cards

Number of players: 2 to 12

The Game:

- The players are given four trigger words relating to goalkeeping. These are:

  1 = Keeper's 2 = Away 3 = Stand up 4 = Tackle

- The players jog randomly in a marked square.

- The coach calls out 1, 2, 3 or 4 and the players react as quickly as possible to the number called.

- For example, if the coach calls out "1", the players shout "Keeper".

- If the coach calls out "3", the players shout "Stand up" and so on.

- In order to maintain concentration, the coach should keep changing the number and corresponding trigger word.

Progression

- In order to enhance sports vision, the coach holds up tach cards instead of calling out numbers.

- The cards could be letters (A,B,C,D), numbers (1,2,3,4), colours (red, blue, yellow, green) or shapes (triangle, diagonal, square, circle), which equate to the correct trigger word.

- The players have to look for the tach cards whilst moving around the field.

- This will further help develop and enhance sports vision.

Exercise 158 >>>>>>

Equipment: 1 goal and 10 footballs

Number of players: 4 goalkeepers and 1 server

The Game:

- One goalkeeper works whilst the other players stand next to the goal and act as observers.

- The server crosses a ball and the goalkeeper either shouts 'keeper's' and comes to catch it or shouts 'away' if he feels the ball is not within his reach.

- After each ball is served and a decision made by the working goalkeeper, the three observers comment on whether they think it was the correct decision.

- After all the balls have been served, change the working goalkeeper.

- It is important that the service is varied.

- When all the players have received the ball from one side, change to serving from the other side.

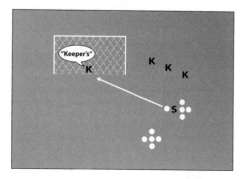

Exercise 159 〉〉〉〉〉

Equipment: 1 goal and 10 footballs

Number of players: 3 + a server

The Game:

- Three players take turns acting as goalkeeper, attacker and defender.

- The server is positioned just outside the penalty area, with 10 footballs.

- He passes to the attacker, who immediately dribbles at the defender.

- At this point, the goalkeeper tells the defender to 'stand up'.

- Only when the ball is out of the attacker's feet does the goalkeeper tell the defender to tackle.

- It is essential the defender doesn't get caught in stride, as the attacker touches the ball, since the attacker can exploit the defender's inability to change direction at this moment.

- The visual clue for the defender and goalkeeper is to look for long, stray touches by the attacker, which allows the defender to move forward and tackle.

- After 10 attacks, the players change roles.

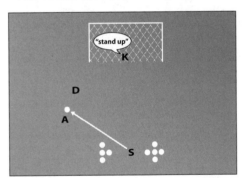

Exercise 160 〉〉〉〉〉

Equipment: 1 goal and 10 footballs

Number of players: 3 + a server

The Game:

- The two previous exercises are now combined.

- The server crosses a ball and the goalkeeper either shouts 'keeper's' and comes to catch it or shouts 'away' if he feels the ball is not within his reach.

- If he claims the ball, he immediately throws to the attacker, who takes on the defender and attempts to score.

- The goalkeeper continually gives instructions to the defender on when to stand and when to tackle.

- If he does not come to claim the ball and shouts 'away', the game becomes alive and the defender attempts to clear.

- When all the balls have been served, change roles.

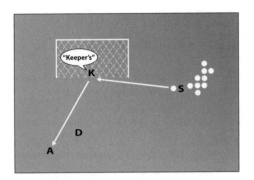

Exercise 161 〉〉〉〉〉

Equipment: 4 cones, 2 goals, balls and a set of bibs

Number of players: 8 + 2 keepers

Dimensions: 50m x 40m

The Game:

- 4 v 4 plus two goalkeepers.

- Play a normal game but ONLY the goalkeepers are allowed to talk.

- Each goalkeeper must continually communicate and keep his team organized.

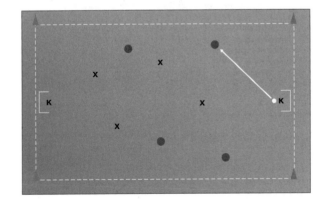

Conclusion

From our research, we suggest that football players should consult a trained professional to undergo and then maintain an appropriate screening programme. If a visual problem is identified, then the necessary corrective action should take place and a training programme implemented. Once this has been carried out, further improvements will only come from sport-specific training programmes which optimise the use of visual information and develop the players' perceptual skills. Certainly, football players do not have to possess supranormal levels of vision to compete at an élite level. In fact, the consensus is that there is no difference in basic visual function between the expert footballer and the novice - just in how the specific visual information is interpreted and then used to define the action.

Recently a number of products, including computer programmes, flashing lights, flashbeams and coloured glasses, have become available to assist in visual training for sport. However, many of these are simply ideas obtained from optometrists and the problem of transfer and specificity must be raised. We do not feel that they place the visual system or the individual under the same visual and physical stress as experienced in a competitive or training environment. We therefore believe these visual training methods are ineffective and will do little to improve soccer performance.

The visual system is the major sensory system, providing over 90% of the information processed by a player. In fact, the visual system dominates the other sensory systems and the brain will always treat the visual information as correct where there is a discrepancy between the eyes and those other systems.

In truth, the effectiveness of visual training is still unknown. Therefore, in light of the current information, our aim must be to create football-specific training programmes which optimise the use of visual information and develop the players' perception, spatial awareness, peripheral vision and decision-making. In football, it is most important to identify and recognise the stimuli in the external field of vision – teammates or opponents. It is essential that players do not just focus on the ball, because if they do, they will not be sufficiently aware of either teammates or opponents! This will lead to slow or incorrect decision-making. We must always create a 'game environment' that simulates the game itself and helps players identify the external stimuli which will enable them to make correct decisions!

However, although visual information guides our motor actions, the visual system alone is insufficient and needs the support and involvement of the other sensory systems, particularly the vestibular and proprioceptive. The reason that football provides a massive challenge to the visual and other systems is that a player has so many options from which to choose. However, many of these decisions and subsequent movements are made whilst off-balance, standing on one leg, jumping, being marked by an opponent, playing on a slippery surface or dealing with the elements. Unlike in other sports such as swimming, running, cycling and rowing, where movements are sequential, a footballer often has to make multiple movements at the same time. For example, when a player is shielding a ball from an opponent, he uses many different body parts, whilst trying to keep possession. The movements in football often involve the whole body, thereby increasing the difficulty and making it harder to be precise. Training must, therefore, always be specific and must push players beyond the parameters that are required for a match.

We believe the exercises in this book will improve an individual's understanding of time and space and provide the cues which will enable a player to take appropriate action in a variety of complex situations. In order to improve the visual system, we have enhanced the use of colour, created pitches of different shapes and sizes, placed goals in different positions on the field, stimulated peripheral vision with the use of two footballs, developed exercises for pre- and post scanning, used inner tubes, eye patches and hopping games to improve unipodalic balance, combined dribbling with space perception and created random agility tag games. We want to turn all young players into potential decision-makers by improving their visual search strategies, which, in turn, will enable them to execute their movements more effectively in a game. We believe that only games such as ours, which use specific situations of play, will achieve this.

For the football coach there is constant pressure to reinvigorate training with new, innovative and challenging training sessions, which address the sport-specific needs of their players. We hope the exercises in this book will provide fun and enjoyment for players, and at the same time introduce a new dimension into training, which challenges and loads the visual system. We also feel this book is just a starting point, since soccer is evolving all the time and coaches need to adapt to ever-changing demands in order to stay one step ahead. We hope coaches will use the above games and develop and adapt them to their own teams. With a little creativity and imagination, they might even take them in a different direction. It is essential that coaches keep up to date with new methods but refine and adapt them to their own beliefs and philosophy. This is the best way of stimulating players and encouraging them to face new situations.

"The intelligent man is one who has successfully fulfilled many accomplishments, and yet is willing to learn more."
Ed Parker

Postscript

Alan 'Sid' Dixon

Whilst on holiday in Spain, I was lucky enough to meet Alan 'Sid' Dixon, who was a professional footballer with Sheffield United, Bristol City, Peterborough and Darlington between 1951 and 1961. Unfortunately, a broken leg brought his professional career to a sudden end and he is still suffering the consequences of that injury. Sid played alongside such famous names as Jimmy Hagan at Sheffield United and John Atyeo at Bristol City. Sid's more famous brother, Johnny, played for Aston Villa. What I wanted to know was how Sid and his brother learnt to play, when growing up in Sheffield.

"During the winter we played football and during the summer it was cricket. We played football whenever and wherever we could. We played in the streets, parks and on any scraps of waste ground that were available. Football in the street was as safe as the park, since the standard of living in Sheffield was low and very few people could afford to run a car of their own. The only hazards were the occasional broken concrete slab, the curb, lamp posts and the pillar boxes. However, they didn't discourage us from playing there every night and at weekends, and football became an obsession for me and my friends.

We used to call it 'coats down' football as we threw down jumpers or coats for goals, set up a pitch and just played. It could be anything from 3 v 3, 4 v 4 or 15 v 15. Looking back, I feel we gained most when it was five aside and that is how I would encourage youngsters to learn today. Most of the kids were my own age group, so not only did we play at home but we also kicked a ball about on the way to school and in the yard at break and lunch times. We were also lucky enough to have a school team in both the primary and secondary schools we attended, so that gave us a further chance to develop our game. Let's be fair, it was also the only escape we had from the grinding poverty of Sheffield just after the war.

If the numbers were small, we played a game of 'poppin' in'. We put bags or coats down for a goal, placed a keeper in between the posts and took it in turns to shoot at him. The first player to score three goals then became the new goalkeeper. This was not so easy as it sounds as we always played with a size 4 or size 5 football and if it got wet or muddy, then it became heavier and heavier and almost impossible to kick (especially in our big, heavy boots that weighed a ton). Either that or the ball became scratched and ripped after being kicked about on the concrete. Heading could also be traumatic, particularly if the ball was heavy and you connected with the lace!

The best thing about it was that we learnt to play football by playing football. There were no adults to tell us what to do, as we transformed the pitches into Hillsborough or Bramall Lane. We developed our own games and our own routines and we attempted to copy the tricks of players like Stanley Matthews or Jimmy Hagan. Most importantly, we learnt how to pass, kick with both feet, ride tackles, muscle players off the ball and tackle hard and our balance was excellent, as we had no desire to fall down on the concrete. We would spend hours talking about the kick around or the next school game coming up. It was our life and cricket got the same treatment in the summer. Basically, we were self-taught and it wasn't until I became a professional that I got coaching for the first time."

This was how most footballers learnt to play in the 40s, 50s and 60s and this system produced many world class players. Obviously, the situation has changed considerably since Sid grew up in Sheffield, but what are the essential conditions needed for football expertise? To us, it seems obvious that we should devote more practice time to the enhancement of attributes such as pattern recognition (reading the play) and game sense, which are clearly essential for expert performance.

As we have emphasised many times in this book, visual training and football intelligence should be developed through a series of small-sided games, where each player has to face and solve a series of problems which are aimed at his physical, technical and mental capacities. Without realising it, Sid and his contemporaries developed excellent pattern recognition, perception and game sense, simply by playing so many 'pick up' games when they were young. In other words, they taught themselves how to play. Is there a lesson for all coaches here?

Alan Ball

Sadly, when this book was near completion, I learnt of the death of Alan Ball, a colleague and a friend. At the peak of his career, he was arguably the best one- and two-touch player in the world. He had a brilliant sense of space, his peripheral visual awareness was second to none and he knew what he was going to do with the ball, three or four moves ahead. I once asked him how he developed this great vision and he summed it up in one word - "practice". Most afternoons he would return to the training ground, with several of the other players and work on one- and two-touch passing. Players would play balls into him at all different heights, speeds and angles and he would quickly glance over his shoulder, looking for the runs of Ray (Kennedy) and John (Radford) and then attempt to pass the ball, first time, into their running paths. There is no doubt that Alan was working on Sports Vision, without realising it, but it helped enhance his performances and gave him an important edge over his fellow professionals. He truly had a vision for football – in the literal sense!

"The soccer of the past we have to respect, the soccer of today we must study, and the soccer of the future we must anticipate."

Bibliography

1. **Sesam Atlas van de Fysiologie.** Silbernagl S and Despopoulos A. Bosch en Keuning nv, Baarn, The Netherlands, 1981.

2. **Color Atlas of Physiology.** Silbernagl S and Despopoulos A. Georg Thieme Verlag, Stutgart, Germany, 5th edition.

3. **Best and Taylor's Physiological Basis of Medical Practice.** 11th Edition. West JB. Williams and Wilkins, Baltimore 1985.

4. **Gray's Anatomy. 37th Edition.** Williams PL, Warwick R, Dyson M, Bannister LH. Churchill Livingstone, London. 1989.

5. **Functionele Neurologie.** Vakaet L Department of Anatomy, Faculty of Medicine, Rijksuniversiteit Gent, Gent, Belgium. 1984.

6. **Correlative Neuroanatomy and Functional Neurology.** Chusid JD. Lang Medical Publications, Los Altos, California, USA. 1970.

7. **Reading the play in team sports.** Damian Farrow, Australian Institute of Sport. Sports Coach Vol 27 No 3 2004.

8. **Sports Expertise: From Theory To Practice.** Bruce Abernethy, University of Queensland: Sports Coach Vol 27 No 3

9. **Developing Game Sense.** Cadeyrn Gaskin and Andrew Martin, Department of Management, Massey University.

10. **Revisit 'Game Sense'.** Alan Launder, Sports Coach.

11. **Can Visual Training Enhance Sporting Performance?** David Mann and Adam Gorman. Sports Coach Vol 28 No 1.

12. **Conditioning the Visual System. A Practical Perspective on Visual Conditioning in Rugby Football.** Rudi Meir, South Cross University, New South Wales.

13. **Improving Reaction Time.** Georgia Tech Sports Sports Medicine and Performance Newsletter 3/12/2001.

14. **Reactive agility—the forgotten aspect of training agility in team sports.** Lyndell Bruce, Damian Farrow and Warren Young, University of Ballarat. Sports Coach Vol 27 No 3.

15. **Visual Search Strategy and Anticipation in Sport.** Mark Williams and Keith Davids, Coaching Focus, No 26 1994.

16. **How Do You Coach Decision-Making?** Jon Royce, Coaching Focus, No 26 1994.

17. **Perception and Action in Sport.** Keith Davids and Craig Handford, Coaching Focus, No 26 1994.

18. **The Contribution of Vision to the Learning and Performance of Sports Skills.** Noel L Blundell, Confederation of Australian Sport, Melbourne.

19. **The Impact of Vision Training on Sports Performance.** Duane Knudson, Baylor University and Darlene A Kluka, University of Oklahoma. JOPARD April 1997.

20. **Selective Attention in Fast Ball Sports. Expert-Novice differences.** B Abernethy. Australian Journal of Science and Medicine in Sport. Dec 1997 Vol 19 No 4.

21. **Understanding Sports Vision.** Dr Jack Gardner. Performance Soccer Conditioning Vol 7 No 5.

22. **Balance Training in a Soccer Strength and Conditioning Programme.** Allen Hendrick, US Air Force Academy. Performance Soccer Conditioning Vol 8 No 5.

23. **Practice, instruction and skill acquisition in soccer: Challenging tradition.** A. Mark Williams, John Moores University, Liverpool and Nicola J. Hodges, University of British Columbia. Journal of Sports Sciences, June 2005; 23(6): 637-650.

24. **Another bad day at the training ground: coping with ambiguity in the coaching context.** Robyn Jones and Mike Wallace, University of Bath, UK. Sport, Education and Society Vol 10, No 1, March 2005.

25. **The Right Brain.** Thomas R Blakeslee Macmillan Press 1980.

26. **La Vision De Juego En El Futbolista.** Luis Fradua Uriondo. Editorial Pandotribo.

27. **Better Vision Naturally.** Wolfgang Rosenbauer.

28. **Developing Game Intelligence in Soccer.** Horst Wein. Reedswain 2004.

29. **Training for Speed, Agility and Quickness.** Lee E. Brown and Vance A. Ferrigno, Human Kinetics 2005.

30. **Coaching Soccer 10-15 year olds.** Stefano Bonaccorso. Reedswain 2001.

31. **Recognising the Moment to Play.** Wayne Harrison, Reedswain 2002.

32. **Assessment of secondary school students' decision-making and game-play ability in soccer.** Minna Blomqvist, Tomi Vanttinen and Pekka Luhtanen. Research Institute for Olympic Sports, Jyvaskyla, Finland.

33. **Agility literature review: Classifications, training and testing.** J. M. Sheppard and W. B Young. Australian Institute of Sport and School of Human Movement and Sport Sciences, University of Ballarat. Journal of Sports Sciences, September 2006.

34. **Improvements in performance following optometric vision therapy in a child with dyspraxia.** Hurst Cm, Van de Weyer S, Smith C, Adler PM. Ophtalmic Physiol Opt 2006:26(2): 199 - 210.

35. **Reading the Game.** Evans L. Coaching Edge, issue 5, Autumn 2006: 20 – 21.

36. **Sport Vision & Performance Analysis.** Griffiths G and Court M. The FA Coaches Association Journal, Spring/Summer 2005: 41- 44.

37. **Sportsvision, Training for Better Performance.** Wilson TA, Falkel J. Human Kinetics, Champaign, USA. 2004.

About the Authors

Jark J D Bosma

Jark Bosma is a Dutch national who works as a consultant neurosurgeon in Sheffield. He did his basic medical training at the State University of Ghent (Belgium) obtaining his MD in 1990. His postgraduate training was largely based in England. This included a year of training in the West Midlands Centre for Spinal Injuries, and a further six months at the Spinal Surgery Unit in Oswestry. He spent a further six months in neurology in the Walton Centre for Neurology and Neurosurgery in Liverpool and following completion of basic surgical training he passed his FRCSEd examination in 1995. After this he joined the neurosurgical training program at The Walton Centre and he passed his FRCS(SN) neurosurgical specialty examination in 2000. He worked briefly in Spinal Orthopaedic surgery in Zürich (Switzerland) in 2001. His subspecialty interest is spinal neurosurgery. He has written a number of scientific publications. Largely because of his involvement in sports through his children and through the interesting and thought provoking discussions with Mick Critchell, he has become increasingly interested in sports medicine and training methods.

Mick Critchell

Certificate of Education (University of Oxford)

Certificate of Physical Education (University of Leeds and Carnegie College)

Head of Year and Head of Physical Education, Harriet Costello School, Basingstoke

Coach and Fitness Adviser to Farnborough Town FC and Basingstoke Town FC

In-service Trainer for Liverpool FC, Fulham FC, Middlesbrough FC, Watford FC, Wycombe Wanderers FC

In-service Trainer for Swedish FA

In-service Trainer for Sports Colleges

Coach, School of Excellence, Portsmouth FC

Coach Educator for Hampshire FA

Author: "300 Innovative Soccer Drills for Total Player Development"

Author: "Warm Ups for Soccer—A Dynamic Approach"

Co-presenter of video: "Going for Goal"

Director, The Football Garage. An approved centre for 1st 4 Sport

Fitness Adviser to several professional footballers.

Keith Granger

UEFA qualified goalkeeping coach

UEFA qualified outfield coach

Professional goalkeeper with Southampton, Darlington and Maidstone. Retired through injury.

Tutor trainer for Football Association

Worked with Martin Thomas, the National Goalkeeping Coach

Goalkeeping coach for Southampton, working with 1st team, the Academy and Development Centres

In-service Trainer for Southampton FC, Liverpool FC, Middlesbrough FC

In-service Trainer for Swedish FA and Finnish FA

Director, The Football Garage. An approved centre for 1st 4 Sport

From left to right Mick Critchell in discussion with Keith Granger and Jark J D Bosma